Me...
for E...

Other titles by the same author

Life Cycles – Astrology and Inner Space
A Guide to Ancient Britain
Crystal Clear (meditation/relaxation tape)

Meditation
for Every Day

INCLUDES OVER 100 INSPIRING MEDITATIONS FOR BUSY PEOPLE

Bill Anderton

PIATKUS

The meditation experience is a world of relaxation, contentment and even a little enlightenment for good measure.

First published in 1995 by
Judy Piatkus (Publishers) Ltd
5 Windmill Street, London W1P 1HF

Reprinted 1996

The moral right of the author has been asserted

A catalogue record for this book
is available from the British Library

ISBN 0–7499–1485–8

Edited by Esther Jagger
Designed by Sue Ryall
Illustrations by One-Eleven Line Art

Set in 11/13 Sabon by
Phoenix Photosetting, Chatham, Kent
Printed and bound in Great Britain by
Biddles Ltd, Guildford and King's Lynn

CONTENTS

INTRODUCTION

The purpose of this book is to provide you with enough information, inspiration and support to be able to meditate successfully. Many people who wish to meditate need to feel confident that what they are doing is correct, so answers to all the common questions are covered. More than this, you will need lots of different ideas to stimulate and maintain your interest, so not only has appropriate information been included, but also many meditations for you to try out.

The book's main focus is to act as a teacher, in just the same way that the leader of a meditation group might do, by providing instruction and feedback. Although it is graded to present a full course in meditation that you can work through from beginning to end, you can also use the contents to build up your own work programme of meditations to suit your particular needs.

Three further points about the content are important. First, the book employs a technique which is suitable for busy, mentally active people in the Western world. The aim is to become an observer of whatever might fill your conscious awareness – thoughts, feelings, sensations and images – and through this to learn more about the inner experience of yourself.

Secondly, the meditations will take you through two levels of experience. The first level is one of relaxation and relieving stress, the most immediate benefits of meditation. This leads on to a healing, calming experience of feeling good about life and oneself. The second level is one of finding out more about oneself through meditation. This is achieved through a series of gentle, guided inner journeys.

Thirdly, most books on meditation begin with the theory and then move on to the practice, but I want to do it the other way round and launch you straightaway into the experience of relaxation and then meditation. The process that you will go through as the book unfolds will take you deeper and deeper into the meditation experience. Much of what I will say and the new ideas that I will introduce will only make sense to you if you have experienced them. It is not an intellectual understanding that we are aiming at, but the wonderful experience that meditation can bring.

Chapter 10 is a question-and-answer session which covers all the common situations and queries that might occur to you. Some of the topics are also discussed in the text, but this chapter is intended as a quick source of reference. Feel free to dip into it at any time.

The book contains lots of meditations to try and some of them are quite lengthy. For the shorter ones, you should have no problem remembering what I suggest you do, but the longer ones may prove more difficult to remember. These are therefore presented in full, with appropriate pauses indicated, as well as some suggested lengths of time to conduct each meditation. I stress the word 'suggested' as it is more important for you to develop a sequence with which you feel comfortable. Because the meditation texts are given in full, it will be easy for you to record them on to a cassette tape to create your own guided meditations. Some people, however, don't respond well to the sound of their own voice, so you might want to ask someone else to make the recording for you.

You can select from the meditations the ones that appeal to

you and develop your own programme. I have also created in Chapter 11 a programme which enables you either to pick-'n'mix or to undergo a more disciplined graded sequence. This programme simply follows the sequence of meditations as they are introduced throughout the book, so you can also use it as a detailed contents list to find particular meditations that interest you.

This book can be used first of all to start you on the right path by describing the techniques of the meditation experience and answering the questions that will occur to you. Then you can use it as a source of inspiration, either dipping in to sample the meditations that appeal to you, or using the book as the basis for a sequence of meditations over a period of time. The approach therefore combines a teaching manual, a source of inspiration and a workbook.

BILL ANDERTON

1

OPENING UP AND
ENTERING IN

Among the many benefits that may be obtained from meditation are self-discovery; spiritual renewal; inner peace; healing, both for yourself and for others; improved relationships, both with others and with yourself; stress control and release; freedom from the fear of death; and acceptance of life. But most important of all is a sense of well-being and belonging, a feeling of being at ease with yourself and with your life.

A common instruction given by meditation group teachers is: 'Now clear your mind of all thoughts and strife.' But it is not easy to clear your mind in this way. As soon as you try to do so, thoughts may jump in: 'Did I leave the car lights on?' . . . 'What am I supposed to think about?' . . . 'This can't be right – I'm thinking about thinking about nothing!' If this sounds like you, read on.

Some meditation techniques are associated with oriental cultures and are not always suitable for the Western way of looking at the world, nor its lifestyle. This is not just a matter of philosophy or religion, but of tradition – what we are used to. You will find that the technique used in this book encourages your mind to be creative, rather than attempting to empty it. Stillness, quiet and calm can be reached through creativity. This is achieved by becoming a dispassionate observer of yourself, your thoughts, feelings and fantasies, rather than being caught up in them as we are during our normal everyday awareness. It is a process of expansion of consciousness and is what I mean by the meditation experience.

Some people can meditate naturally, or intuitively. Others have to learn how to do it. When you have used this book for a while, you should be able to meditate naturally and without effort. You could also benefit from attending a group and following the advice of its leader. In Chapter 11 you will find advice on how to set up and run your own meditation group, for meditation can be either a lone occupation or a social one. The rest of this book is designed so that you can work on your own, or in a group, or even as a family unit. When you try the course of meditations and practical exercises presented, work gently through the system. The meditations have been carefully graded to enable you to make a safe progression. An unfolding will then take place, rather as a flower will bloom after being given proper nourishment and when the time is right.

Before moving on to the meditation exercises, a programme of relaxation will benefit you greatly. It does not matter whether you are considering meditating on your own or with a group. What *is* essential is that you should be able to relax fully before you meditate, although the meditation itself will relax you.

First of all you must release the tensions in both your body and mind. Try this practical technique, which works well for most people.

Relaxation

RELAXATION SEQUENCE

– Assume a posture that is comfortable and which you can maintain throughout your meditation (more will be said later about the effects of good posture). Wear loose-fitting clothes, with no jewellery or other items that might restrict your circulation or distract your attention. It is helpful to develop a certain amount of regularity or ritual in your meditation exercises. To heighten this sense you might wear the same clothes, adopt the same posture and sit or lie in the same place each time. Sitting upright, or lying down, or adopting a comfortable yoga posture are all suitable.

— Make sure that your spine is straight and under no pressure. If you have a weakness in your back, make sure it is supported, for instance by a chair back. Lying down gives support to all parts of your body.

— Relax! It's easier said than done, so take positive action with the following steps.

— Let your hands lie open; your legs can be either apart or crossed below the knees. Let your breathing be steady and slightly deeper than normal, but not much. What is essential is each breath in should last the same length of time as each breath out. Let us suppose that, as you breathe in, you count up to five. When you exhale you must also count to five. It does not matter what the exact count is, as long as intake and output are even. What you should be aiming for is a regular *rhythm* with which you feel comfortable. Nothing about relaxation should be stressful. You will find that the simple act of breathing slightly deeper than normal is enough to relax you to a certain extent. Encourage this process by imagining stress and tension flowing out from you as you breathe out.

— Drain your body of all tension. Do this by focusing on and *tensing* each part of your body in turn, and then allow it to relax. Start with your head and neck. Focus on the tension, then let it flow from your head and neck, down through your shoulders and both arms. You will feel the dross travelling down your arms to your hands. Do not check the flow; let the tension stream out through your fingers. Or imagine that your breath takes away the tension, as suggested above.

Yes, it works! Fuller and deeper relaxation sequences are given on pages 17 and 25.

You should now be in a relaxed state. However, if you find that your mind is over-active, which will not be conducive to meditation, try thinking about something you enjoy which brings a feeling of peace and relaxation. Examples of suitable subjects for reflection in this way are a gentle riverside view, a country garden, a tree, flowers or perhaps the sea – whatever gives you a sense of quiet and security. Soothing music may also help you, or natural sounds such as the sea, rain falling or birdsong. You can buy cassette tapes of these sounds (see Chapter 11 for information about aids to relaxation).

Reflection is not concentration. Your thoughts should be light, musing and not too deep. Regard the subject of your reflection from various directions; new aspects may well show themselves as your viewpoint or perspective changes.

Don't try to suppress your thoughts, but watch them. Allow a thought to come into your mind. Look at it, be aware of it, watch it, then allow it to disappear and wait for the next thought to appear. In this way you become detached from your thoughts, an observer rather than someone who is caught up in them. Extricating yourself from your thought processes to become a passive observer is a relaxing exercise in itself, and an effective technique for stress relief. The same method can be applied to your feelings, so that you become an observer of all aspects of yourself.

You can deal with worrying thoughts and feelings not by trying to suppress them, but by watching them, and allowing them to go from your mind when they are ready. This is a process of release. Suppressed thoughts and feelings, particularly bad ones such as anger or frustration, are not a good thing, and can eventually create a negative reaction on your well-being and health.

You can extend this observer role by becoming aware of your body too. Don't ignore any cramps or tensions, but focus on them. Watch them, live with them, be aware of them . . . allow them to flow away, and then shift your centre of attention to a new focus. The aim should be to find eventually a still, unmoving focus or centre of attention. This will occur when you are completely relaxed and when your mind is still. As with a pool of water that has been turbulent and becomes still, you will then be ready to see below the surface.

Starting to Meditate

The aim of meditation is to create *relaxed awareness*. Usually, we are only fully relaxed when asleep – and only fully aware when in a state of adrenalin-pumped tension. Relaxation and heightened awareness are not often experienced together. But meditation brings them together, and the experience is quite different from either normal wakefulness or sleep. To achieve this state, direct your attention inwards so that you become an observer of yourself, of your thoughts, feelings and sensations. Try this:

OBSERVING ONESELF

– Relax, as described in the relaxation sequence on page 5.

– Become aware of your thoughts.

– Pause (*20 seconds*).

– Just let your thoughts arise in your mind. Watch them and then allow them to slip away.

– Pause (*20 seconds*).

– Allow another thought to arise and then slip away. Note your thoughts carefully. What is it that is on your mind?

– Pause (*20 seconds*).

– Become aware of your feelings.

– Pause (*20 seconds*).

– How are you feeling today? Happy? Sad? Bored? Irritated? Inspired?

– Pause (*20 seconds*).

– Simply become aware of how you are feeling, and allow the feeling to grow. Become an observer of your feelings, then let them slip away. Take careful note of how you are feeling today.

– Pause (*20 seconds*).

– Become aware of your sensations. is there any part of your body that particularly draws your attention? Become aware of it and simply observe the sensation.

– Pause (*20 seconds*).

– Are there any other sensations that attract your attention? Allow them to come into your awareness and take careful note of them. Then let them go.

– Pause (*20 seconds*).

– Breathe slightly deeper than normal, then open your eyes.

You will see from this meditation that the aim is not to get rid of thoughts, feelings and sensations and to become empty, but in this instance to allow them *to flow* unhindered and to be a non-judgemental, non-critical observer of them. You can then begin to explore the nature of these inner experiences. Why do you have these particular thoughts, feelings and sensations? Where do they come from? What are they trying to say to you? What is it that you, your mind, your body, need? You may surprise yourself. Don't *try* to find out the answers to these questions, just observe yourself. Doing this invokes the relaxation response. Enjoy your self.

Breathing and Relaxation

There is a simple breathing technique which is a key to relaxation and which opens up the meditation experience. Most teachers of oriental forms of meditation talk about it. The action of breathing is usually an unconscious one, but if we wish to we can control it, breathe more deeply, more quickly, more slowly, even stop breathing for a few seconds. It is a process vital to our life and health, with a natural rhythm, and through it we are constantly in touch with the surrounding atmosphere. To become aware of your experience of your own breathing, try this:

COUNTING BREATHS

— Relax, as described in the relaxation sequence on page 5.

— Focus your attention on your breathing.

— Breathe a little more deeply than normal.

— As you breathe in, count to yourself from one to five. (The length of the count at each stage is up to you – do whatever fits your natural rhythm.)

– Hold your breath for a count of three.

– Breathe out and count to yourself from one to five.

– Hold your breath for a count of three.

– Repeat from beginning several times.

– Continue, but, as you breathe out, instead of counting say to yourself: 'Relax.'

– Do this several times for a further minute or so.

– When you are ready, end the meditation by observing how you feel, becoming aware of your body again, and then opening your eyes.

The effects of this meditation are to make you aware of your inner, unconscious processes, especially the process of breathing. From the point of view of expanding awareness it will make you aware of the significance of breathing as something with a rhythm that supports the whole of the life force. Becoming aware of your breathing and controlling it in this way is also a method of relieving stress, of relaxing and attuning to the supportive life force.

In the exercise above I introduced a mantra – a word used as an object for meditation. Mantras can be sounds, single words or phrases, which are repeated in meditation. I have found that the most effective mantras can be positive suggestions that you give to yourself, such as in this instance the word 'Relax'. You will find more on mantras and positive thinking in Chapter 2 (see also page 224).

In the full relaxation sequence on page 25 you will use your breathing to clear out any tension and stress locked away in your body. This is achieved by imaging that your out-breath carries the tension away with it. You'll see what I mean when we get there. But first we must look at the important question of posture.

Posture

The correct posture is quite simply one in which you feel comfortable. Another important characteristic is that your posture should be open and expansive, with no parts of your body squashed or crushed. The most important area in which to adopt this open attitude is your chest and abdomen, so that you can breathe properly. It's no good trying to breathe deeply, rhythmically and freely if you are slouched, which crumples your stomach and the muscles surrounding your diaphragm. Try this:

THE PERFECT POSTURE
10 minutes

— Relaxation sequence (page 5).

— Imagine that sitting with you, or lying beside you if you are lying down, is another person who is meditating with you, and that this person has beautiful poise and posture. Take note of the way their head and body in particular are positioned and start to copy this poise and posture.

— Imagine that you blend with this perfect person so that you begin to experience what the perfect posture feels like for you.

— Feel your whole being expanding as you create a greater sense of space inside yourself. Gradually shift and expand your posture until it is poised, relaxed and openly expanded. Imagine that your body takes up more space than usual by expanding it outwards and upwards, to increase your height.

— You are creating an enlarged sense of inner space.

— Practise the breathing technique on page 10, feeling the extra space inside you into which you can now breathe.

— When you are ready, open your eyes.

My suggestions for posture are to lie down on your back with your head supported on a cushion and your arms down by your sides. Don't cross your legs. Stretch, so that your height increases slightly, and then relax. Alternatively you can sit in a chair which allows you to have a straight back – and therefore an uncramped, open diaphragm area.

In the posture meditation I used the word '*poise*', which means that your body should be in a state of relaxed but alert balance. To achieve this, imagine that your centre of gravity is just below your navel and that, when sitting, all your body weight is directed through this point.

Another tip to help you achieve the right posture while sitting is to imagine that someone is taking hold of the hair on the back of your head and gently pulling it upwards. By following the line of this pull you will move your body so that it expands upwards, your diaphragm and stomach area open up and your back straightens.

Don't go too far, or instead of achieving poise you will become stiff and tense. Poise is achieved when you have found the balance between being over-relaxed or slumped and rigidly stiff and tense. Don't do battle with your muscles – make friends with them! Allow them to be comfortable and to help you achieve the feeling of poise.

The *Alexander Technique* (see page 222) is a system which places a lot of emphasis on posture, which can be analysed and corrected to have an effect on the way we feel about ourselves. In this system the neck should be relaxed and free; the head tilts slightly forward and then eases up; and the back eases up and widens. Practising these movements helps you to expand your body and free your muscles, particularly those in your back which take a lot of the strain of daily activity.

Consciously expanding the back by easing your posture and at the same time widening is ideal for achieving a posture that will encourage rather than cramp the meditation experience. Some *yoga* postures are of course appropriate, but for our purposes sitting or lying are quite adequate, provided you can induce the feeling of openness and poise.

Expanding yourself out of a slumped posture will help you to achieve the goal of relaxed awareness which was first mentioned on page 8. You will also discover that the sense of expansion and poise, leading to relaxed awareness, creates an *inner sense of expansion* – an expanded inner space of awareness. Unless you create this sense of space your meditations will not be very effective and your awareness will not expand.

Gradually, by stages, we are creating an inner workspace, and later the meditations will take place within this workspace. It might not make perfect sense yet, but you will need this inner space in which experiences can come to you, in which new thoughts, feelings, imaginings and awareness can grow and develop.

So correct posture is not just a matter of discipline. It is a way to create both relaxed awareness and an inner workspace for the meditation experience.

To enhance the sensation of relaxed but open awareness, don't clench your fists. Some teachers suggest turning your open palms upwards, but I find that it tenses the muscles in my forearm. If you find this too, keep your palms turned down, perhaps one on each knee if sitting, or by your sides if lying.

I sometimes sit with my left hand cradled in my right. This is symbolic of the active hand (I am right-handed) being made passive by lying under the non-active hand.

If you lie down to meditate you may find it comfortable to support your head with a cushion.

In a sitting position, make sure your back is straight and well supported. Don't slouch because it will cramp the muscles of your abdomen and restrict your breathing.

THE INNER WORKSPACE

— Relaxation sequence (page 5).

— Create the perfect posture.

— Do the Counting Breaths meditation (page 10).

— On an out-breath, say to yourself, 'I am relaxed.'

— On the next out-breath say, 'I am poised.' Sense your centre of gravity when you say this.

— On the next out-breath say, 'I am open.' Sense your awareness of an expanding inner space when you say this.

— Repeat: 'I am relaxed. . . .' Breathe in. Breathe out and say, 'I am poised. . . .' Breathe in. Breathe out and say, 'I am open.'

— Say these to yourself, one on each out-breath, and repeat for a minute or two.

— When you are ready, finish the meditation by becoming aware of your body and your environment, then open your eyes.

I have now introduced relaxation, breathing and posture to you. Relaxation follows from correct breathing and posture; it is created out of the right conditions. We will now delve into the relaxation process a little more deeply.

The Relaxation Response

One effective system for relaxation stress relief is called autogenics (see page 224), and I have adapted its main features for use in the relaxation that occurs before a meditation session.

Below is an autogenic training programme. If all you are interested in is stress relief, I recommend it. It is quite long and therefore unsuitable in its full form as the introduction to a meditation session, but it will stand alone as an effective relaxation technique to which you will respond quickly and easily. All the lines can be repeated for best effect.

A good introduction to autogenics is included in James Hewitt's *The Complete Relaxation Book* (see Recommended Reading on page 247). For the following exercise you should preferably be lying down in a warm, comfortable environment and unlikely to be disturbed for 20 minutes or so. Because the sequence is lengthy, you will either need someone to take you through it, or you should record it on to a cassette tape.

Johannes Schultz, who developed the system of autogenics, emphasised that you need what he termed 'a passive casual attitude'. He said that, 'The system works automatically – you do not do it.'

AUTOGENIC RELAXATION PROGRAMME

Resting comfortably, eyes closed
Breathing easily
Taking slow, deep breaths
Lying with your full weight
Letting go and settling down
Breathing slowly and deeply
Letting tension go
Pulling toes and instep towards face, contracting right leg
    strongly from foot to hip
Letting go from contraction of right leg
Right leg limp and relaxed
Taking easy, deep breaths
Deep easy breathing
Pulling toes and instep towards face, contracting left leg
    strongly from foot to hip
Letting go from contraction of left leg

17

Left leg limp and relaxed

Breathing slowly and deeply

Making a fist with right hand and squeezing tightly, tightening whole area strongly from hand to shoulder

Letting go from contraction, relaxing arm

Right arm limp and relaxed

Taking slow, deep breaths

Making a fist with left hand and squeezing tightly, tightening whole arm strongly from hand to shoulder

Letting go from contraction, relaxing arm

Left arm limp and relaxed

Both arms limp and relaxed from hands to shoulders

Breathing slowly and deeply

Tightening tummy muscles and pressing down with back and head

Letting go from tension in abdomen and upper body

Tension flowing away

Breathing slowly and deeply

Bringing lips together and pressing them together firmly, contracting facial muscles from chin to scalp

Face relaxing and broadening, thinking of smiling

Taking a slow, deep breath

Holding breath and contracting all body muscles from feet to scalp

Letting breath out through mouth, relaxing whole body

Tension flowing out and whole body relaxed and comfortable

Letting go from tension with every breath out

Breathing calm and regular

Lying with full weight and letting go

Relaxed and calm

Letting relaxation happen in body and mind

Letting it happen

Letting attention dwell easily on body parts, visualising each part, letting go from tension, starting with feet

Right foot feeling heavy and relaxed

Left foot feeling heavy and relaxed

Right ankle feeling heavy and relaxed
Left ankle feeling heavy and relaxed
Right calf feeling heavy and relaxed
Left calf feeling heavy and relaxed
Right knee feeling heavy and relaxed
Left knee feeling heavy and relaxed
Right thigh feeling heavy and relaxed
Left thigh feeling heavy and relaxed
Right hip and buttock feeling heavy and relaxed
Left hip and buttock feeling heavy and relaxed
Right leg from foot to hip feeling heavy and relaxed
Left leg from foot to hip feeling heavy and relaxed
Belly below navel and solar plexus above navel feeling comfortable and relaxed
Lower back feeling heavy and relaxed
Chest muscles feeling comfortable and relaxed
Breathing deeply and easily
Ribs feeling free and relaxed
Belly and solar plexus feeling comfortable and relaxed
Upper back feeling heavy and relaxed
Right hand feeling heavy and relaxed
Left hand feeling heavy and relaxed
Right forearm feeling heavy and relaxed
Left forearm feeling heavy and relaxed
Right elbow feeling heavy and relaxed
Left elbow feeling heavy and relaxed
Right upper arm feeling heavy and relaxed
Left upper arm feeling heavy and relaxed
Right shoulder feeling heavy and relaxed
Left shoulder feeling heavy and relaxed
Right arm from hand to shoulder feeling heavy and relaxed
Left arm from hand to shoulder feeling heavy and relaxed
Right hand feeling relaxed and becoming warm
Warmth flowing into right hand
Right hand feeling warm and relaxed
Left hand feeling relaxed and becoming warm
Warmth flowing into left hand

Left hand feeling warm and relaxed
Both hands in warm sunlight
Passively aware of warmth in hands
Letting warmth come
Warmth flowing up right arm
Right lower arm feeling warm and relaxed
Warmth flowing up left arm
Left lower arm feeling warm and relaxed
Warmth flowing through right elbow into upper arm
Right upper arm feeling warm and relaxed
Warmth flowing through left elbow into upper arm
Left upper arm feeling warm and relaxed
Warmth flowing into right shoulder
Right shoulder feeling warm and relaxed
Warmth flowing into left shoulder
Left shoulder feeling warm and relaxed
Right arm from hand to shoulder feeling warm and relaxed
Left arm from hand to shoulder feeling warm and relaxed
Feeling relaxed and peaceful
Pulse calm and strong
Feeling relaxed and peaceful
Pulse calm and strong
Warmth reaching all parts of body
Warmth from shoulders flowing into chest and upper back
Chest feeling warm and relaxed
Upper back feeling warm and relaxed
Breathing calm and regular
Passively aware of breathing
Breathing freely
Breathing calm and regular
Letting breathing happen
Breathing muscles free and relaxed
Letting breathing happen
Being breathed
Breathing calm and relaxed
Warmth flowing into lower back
Lower back feeling warm and relaxed

Solar plexus becoming warm
Solar plexus sun warm
Whole abdomen warm and relaxed
Passively aware and letting warmth happen
Solar plexus warm
Whole abdomen warm and relaxed
Warmth flowing into pelvis and hips
Pelvis and hips warm and relaxed
Warmth flowing into right thigh
Right thigh warm and relaxed
Warmth flowing into left thigh
Left thigh warm and relaxed
Warmth flowing through right knee into lower leg
Right lower leg warm and relaxed
Warmth flowing through left knee into lower leg
Left lower leg warm and relaxed
Warmth flowing through right ankle into foot
Right foot warm and relaxed
Warmth flowing through left ankle into foot
Left foot warm and relaxed
Right leg from foot to hip warm and relaxed
Left leg from foot to hip warm and relaxed
Pelvis and abdomen warm and relaxed
Solar plexus warm and relaxed
Lower back warm and relaxed
Chest muscles warm and relaxed
Upper back warm and relaxed
Right arm from hand to shoulder warm and relaxed
Left arm from hand to shoulder warm and relaxed
Throat and neck becoming warm and relaxed
Whole body from feet to neck feeling warm and relaxed
Warm and relaxed
Mind becoming calm and quiet
Speech muscles relaxed and still
Vision muscles relaxed and still
Mind quiet and serene
Body and mind still and calm

Forehead pleasantly cool
Mind cool and calm
Face muscles relaxed
Body warm and relaxed
Body in warm sunlight, head in cool shade
Pleasant warm sunshine, refreshing cool shade
Arms, legs and trunk heavy, warm and relaxed
Head pleasantly cool
Mind cool and calm
Attention turning inwards
Passively aware of mind relaxed and calm
Forehead pleasantly cool
Mind cool, calm and peaceful
Ready to return now to full wakefulness
Energy filling arms, legs and whole body
All heaviness going
Facial muscles relaxed and alive
Full wakefulness returning on counting back from five to zero
Five – stretching legs and letting go. Four.
Three – stetching arms and legs and letting go. Two.
One – opening eyes, awake, relaxed and feeling well. Zero.

Personality Types

The emphasis in the programme given above is on being *heavy and relaxed*, but there is also another approach – creating the experience of feeling *light and relaxed*.

The feeling-heavy routine suits people with an active, buoyant personality who need to slow down, but for those with a more down-to-earth or even depressed disposition, a better relaxation exercise is to allow your limbs to feel light and airy. Inwardly, you might need to 'lighten up' rather than encourage the feeling of heaviness.

The approach to adopt depends partly on your personality.

Jungian or analytical psychology, founded by Carl Gustav Jung, suggests that there are four main personality types: thinking, feeling, sensing and intuitive. These are similar to the four personality types that in the Middle Ages were described as four 'humours': sanguine (thinking), phlegmatic (feeling), melancholic (sensing) and choleric (intuitive). Also, modern psychological astrology identifies the equivalent personality types as Air (thinking), Water (feeling), Earth (sensing) and Fire (intuitive) types.

I mention these in passing here as it is important when choosing appropriate and effective relaxation sequences and meditations, to choose those that are appropriate for you. Not all of them will be. You will find more about them in Chapter 10.

The Meditation Environment

Creating a conducive inner environment is a theme which runs through the whole of the meditation experience. So far we have been putting the emphasis on creating an inner space or environment, but some emphasis should be placed on the corresponding outer environment. One of the discoveries you may make through meditation is that the apparently clear boundaries between our selves and the outside world are not so clear-cut after all – and that there is a relationship between what we experience inwardly and the events and situations that take place around us.

This is a *holistic view*, in which 'inner' and 'outer' are not clearly divided but have a relationship with one another. Discovering and exploring this relationship is one of the exciting prospects of meditation. It is also one of the reasons why meditation is claimed not to be a passive activity that has no bearing or influence on our outer lives. Indeed, you will find that meditation has a beneficial effect both on yourself and on the circumstances of your life and relationships with others.

The main point is that the environment in which you meditate is worth considering as part of the total experience. It is not necessary always to meditate at the same time and in the same place, although this does have its advantages. Making meditation a *part of everyday life* should be your constant aim; anything that tends to have the opposite effect, treating meditation as something to be kept separate, or even cut off from the daily course of living, should be discouraged. So if you do create a special place and time to meditate, keep this in mind.

Creating a *sense of ritual* and having a ritual space helps you to focus on the meditation itself. Make sure that the room is not too brightly lit and that it is warm — the physiological effects of meditation can make you feel cold and therefore uncomfortable, which is not conducive to relaxation. Make sure you are comfortable and that your clothing is loose and does not constrict you at all. You could choose a particular garment to wear only while you are meditating, and a particular chair, cushion or mat to use for your meditation. Ritual and regularity form a constant backdrop, setting up the conditions within which the inner activity of the meditation experience can take place without distraction.

If possible, make sure that there will be *no disturbances* during your meditation session (remember to take the phone off the hook!) This might not prove easy, especially if there are children around, but if you can't guarantee peace and quiet don't let this be a reason for not meditating. Go ahead anyway. Distractions are at worst only irritating. When you enter a world of relaxed awareness *your senses become heightened and more acute,* which means that the slightest noise can become a distraction. So rather than being put off and getting annoyed, take it as a sign that your meditation is working. Distractions can even be incorporated into your programme and become objects for meditation, as I shall explain in Chapter 2.

In my regular meditation group, it is a standing joke that as soon as we begin to meditate a cacophony of noise will start outside, the seagulls that fly around being a particular distraction. But we realised after a while that the apparent coincidence of noise with our meditations was not a coincidence at all – there was no increase in the general noise level, just in our awareness of it.

You may notice that your tummy always seems to rumble and groan when you meditate, and your mouth begins to salivate. In a group, rumbling tummies and seemingly loud swallowing noises can make you feel embarrassed. No problem. It's normal. It's another sign that you are entering the meditation experience. When you meditate, your respiration and heart rate and their associated physiological functions slow down. This is a signal to the digestion to speed up, hence the grumbling tummy and salivation. Again, to deal with it is simply a matter of increased awareness about what is going on.

To avoid feeling uncomfortable during a meditation and to prevent your digestive system from affecting your respiration and heart rate (these are automatically repressed after eating, which is why a heavy meal makes you feel physically tired), try not to eat within an hour or so of meditating. Don't drink, either, if it will make you want to go to the loo.

Now you are ready to experience a full meditation/relaxation sequence, based on the exercises introduced so far. Here it is in full.

CREATING INNER SPACE
10–15 minutes

– Close your eyes and begin to breathe slightly more deeply than you would normally. Allow your diaphragm to expand as you breathe in. Then, as you breathe out, allow your body tension to flow out with your breath. You can breathe in through your nose and out through your mouth, but you don't have to if you find it difficult. Breathe in again, slightly more deeply than normal, then, as you breathe out, release any tension as you begin to relax. Repeat this pattern, and as you breathe out become more and more relaxed. Allow your breath to do the work.

— Pause.

— Focus your attention on your feet, and relax them. You can do this by first moving them around and then letting them become still. Here's another way to relax your muscles and release body tension: first make the muscles quite tense and tight, and then let them flop as you release the tension. Do this with your feet. Tense them, then . . . release.

— Pause.

— Next, move your attention to your legs. Allow any tension to flow away. Imagine your breath flowing down into your legs as you breathe in. Then relax as you breathe out. Tense your leg muscles up tight . . . then release the tension and relax. All the time becoming more and more relaxed.

— Pause.

— Next, move your attention to your hips and relax them in the same way.

— Pause.

— All the time becoming more relaxed.

— Pause.

— Now turn your attention to the central area of your body, and in particular the area around your stomach and solar

26

plexus. Become aware of how your posture is poised over and through your centre of gravity.

— Pause.

— Become relaxed.

— Pause.

— And now your shoulders and neck.

— Pause.

— Become relaxed.

— Relax your arms and your hands.

— Pause.

— Finally, relax the muscles of your head and face. Let yourself smile a little.

— Pause.

— Enjoy complete relaxation.

— Pause.

— If there is a part of your body that was particularly tense before, then focus on it again and relax it even more.

— Pause.

— Become aware of your breathing again, and practise counting breaths for a while.

— Pause.

— Now become an observer of your thoughts. Don't suppress them, but simply watch them as they crop up in your mind. Watch your thoughts. Take note of them. Then let them slip away. Allow another thought to arise. Observe it . . . then let it slip away. What is it that is on your mind?

— Pause.

— Let it slip away . . . and relax. . . . Place the word 'Peace' in your mind. Meditate on 'Peace'. Let it touch your heart, mind and breath. Peace fills your body within and without. Release the word 'Peace', so that only the spirit of peace remains.

— Pause.

— Become still.

— Pause.

— Now become an observer of your feelings. How are you feeling today? Worried? Bored? Depressed? Happy? What-ever your feelings, simply be aware of them, observing them and allowing them to be. Perhaps another feeling comes into your awareness. Allow it to come. Be aware of it. Then let the feeling go . . . as you become still.

— Pause.

— This is the end of the relaxation sequence. If you wish, you can remain totally relaxed as you lead into one of the later medi-tations, or you can bring your meditation to an end. To do this, become aware of your breathing. Breathe a little more deeply than you would normally. . . . Be aware of your body and of your surroundings . . . then, when you are ready, open your eyes.

The Creating Inner Space meditation can form an introduc-tory sequence for any of the meditations which follow, or you can use it at any time as a stand-alone sequence to induce relaxation, relieve stress and create a feeling of well-being.

Visualisation

Now that you have created an inner workspace, it is time to try your first meditation that includes visualisation – using the imagination to create inner pictures.

ENTERING THE FOREST
20 minutes

– Go through the relaxation sequence called Creating Inner Space (page 25).

– Imagine that you are standing on the edge of a forest looking for a way into it. This is not a forest that you know in your real life, but one that exists inside you, in your imagination.

– Pause.

– Really be there: feel the ground beneath your feet and look around to discover what you can see. Build up the picture in your mind.

– Pause.

– What is the weather like? Can you hear anything – birds singing, perhaps? What time of year is it?

– Pause.

– You can see a way into the forest and decide to enter.

— Pause.

— Don't go far, just into the trees, then stop and absorb the atmosphere and the change of scenery. It has become darker as the trees overshadow you, but you can still see a little way.

— Pause.

— If you wish, you can walk further into the forest and begin to explore it. Become aware in particular of the trees that surround you, their colours and patterns and the atmosphere that they create.

— Pause.

— Choose a particular tree and go up to it. Feel the bark, and be aware of the tree's roots beneath the earth and the branches above.

— Pause.

— Go a little further into the forest to see what you can find.

— Pause.

— When you are ready, retrace your steps until you are once more on the edge of the forest.

— Pause.

— You can return at any time that you wish to continue your exploration.

— Pause.

— To end the meditation, become aware of your breathing. Breathe a little more deeply. Become aware of your body and the place in which you are meditating. When you are ready, stay completely relaxed and open your eyes.

Some people find visualisation very easy, while for others it is harder. Most children can do it with no difficulty at all, and then as they grow older inhibition sets in and the ability disappears.

Many of the meditations which follow incorporate suggestions for creative visualisation. If at first you find it difficult, do persist, as it will become easier. For some people visualisation is not an easy thing to do. If this is you, then no matter; the meditations will still be suitable for you to work through. Instead of visualising images at my suggestion, then allow thoughts, feelings and impressions to arise in you in response to those suggestions. All the following remarks on the significance of inner images apply equally to the thoughts, feelings and impressions that arise instead of – or as well as – images during your meditations.

Communicating with the Unconscious

The unconscious (see page 226) contains all the new possibilities and potential for the future that lie within us. It is the receptacle for all our memories and past experiences. The unconscious is the source of all creative impulses and the sea out of which grows an island of self-awareness which we call the *ego*. We identify ourselves with our ego, but really our whole person includes our unconscious as well as our conscious selves. There is another world of activity going on inside us all the time, of which we are normally completely unaware – unconscious activity.

In meditation we turn inwards towards the unconscious and create an inner space through which its contents can come into our awareness. Meditation opens us up to become aware of all the hidden possibilities and potentials that lie within us. The unconscious contains all these possibilities. Its surface layer houses all our personal memories and experiences which are not in everyday awareness. Deeper in the unconscious lie all the memories and experiences which we share as human beings. Even deeper lie our instinctive animal, physical natures; the memories of our existence throughout the history of our evolution; the deepest layer of the unconscious is our physical body and everything that we regard as external to our selves.

I will explain more about this, but for now the important point is to learn, through meditation, to form a right relationship with the unconscious so that its life-enhancing, creative energies can work positively with us. Without this relationship the creative energy of life is suppressed and can even work against us. Many of life's problems and even some illnesses derive from a poor relationship with the inner promptings of the unconscious.

Meditation makes us more sensitive to and aware of such promptings, which may come through our thoughts and feelings, or directly from the physical body. They can also come through the sort of inner images that were employed in the previous meditation. The unconscious communicates to us through such images. In dreams we have no control over them, but in meditation it is possible to choose the particular images that we wish to work with and explore. The unconscious can then join in and be creative, helping these images to change, grow, move and develop. The trick is to get the ball rolling by setting up a particular image and then letting the creative process take over. When this is occurring, you should accept whatever images come to you without question or censorship, even if they seem trite or obvious. Simply act as an observer, in the same way as you observe your thoughts, feelings and sensations.

Symbols and archetypes

The images of visualisation in meditation are *symbols*, pregnant with meaning. Symbols have an *archetypal quality*, i.e. a particular symbol has a meaning independent of the particular individual who creates or experiences it. (See pages 227–8 for more on symbols and archetypes.) The meaning of the archetypal aspect of symbols can be discovered from the associations made about them by the culture in which we live, or previous cultures and their mythologies.

For example, an archetypal meaning attached to or associated with a snake or serpent might be the idea of wisdom or intuitive knowledge. A rose signifies love and a butterfly new birth, and so on. These archetypal meanings are helpful in choosing an appropriate symbol or image with which to work in meditation, but they are less helpful when it comes to interpreting images that occur spontaneously in meditation.

Symbols experienced in this way can have personal significance which may have little to do with the archetypal meaning. Also, one person's feelings about or attitude to the same image may be very different. What matters is how *you* respond to a symbol or image, and not what a book might tell you is the particular meaning.

These images should not necessarily be understood in a literal sense, and their surface meaning can even be misleading. The right attitude is to become an observer of the inner world of your imagination and allow the images to unfold as they will. I described symbols as 'pregnant with meaning', which suggests that, once they are visualised, their meaning has yet to come forth and be born; in time they will reveal their significance and present you with an opportunity for exploration, a way into deepening your meditation. Immediate definitions and interpretations leave no room for further expansion of awareness and the images will lose their life. Allow them to grow, change and evolve.

Images associated with finding a way in are potent gateways to expanded awareness. Such images include mirrors, doorways, caves, water and tunnels. Picture yourself in meditation looking into one of these or passing into one – going through a doorway, for example – and you will automatically find your meditation deepening.

The particular image that I used in the previous meditation was a forest. Entering a forest is a symbol for entering into the magical, fairytale world of the unconscious, where the normal laws of the universe are suspended and the laws of mythology, fairytales and the imagination hold sway. In the various medieval legends about the search for the Holy Grail, we are told how each knight of the Round Table departed separately from King Arthur's castle: 'Each one went the way upon which he had decided, and they set out into the forest at one point and another, there where they saw it to be thickest.' In this way, each knight would experience his own unique, personal adventure.

An inward journey

It is, of course, still possible today to conduct a heroic quest in the world, but our quest lies inward. In embarking on the meditation journey, you are beginning your own unique adventure. The unconscious offers the image of the Grail as your goal, a cup of infinite spiritual treasures. The first step is to enter the forest, to commit yourself to the journey. Your own goals may be less fanciful than the Holy Grail, but whatever you have in mind, the journey towards achieving them has now begun.

This chapter has looked at the basics of meditation – the practice of relaxed awareness and the technique of becoming an observer of yourself. Chapter 2 takes this a step further by introducing meditations for people with a busy or stressful lifestyle. It also expands on the use of mantras and positive thinking, as well as helping you to develop an awareness of your inner landscape as an inspiring source of inner wisdom.

2

MEDITATION THE WESTERN WAY

Do you recognise any of the following?

'*I never seem to have time for myself.*'

'*I want to meditate, but it would be too time-consuming.*'

'*I would like to meditate, but there are always distractions.*'

'*I am very active, and meditation would be boring for me.*'

'*The demands put on me by other people mean that I can't find the time or space to meditate. There always seem to be more important things to do.*'

'*Meditation would help me to unwind, but by the end of the day I'm so tired all I want is to put my feet up and watch TV.*'

These are all comments made by people who lead busy lives, who have demands put on them by work or family, who have time-consuming and stressful demands made of them, who have responsibilities and commitments that don't enable them to put themselves – yourself – first. These are typical characteristics of a busy Western lifestyle, which you probably experience for yourself on a daily basis. Full-time education, work, career, family life and bringing up children are all demanding situations which require us to give ourselves 100 per cent to them, even if we don't or can't live up to this demand.

So on the surface there would seem to be some conflict between the Western lifestyle and meditation, which asks you to set aside often unavailable time on a regular basis, and then to forget the demands of the outside world and focus entirely on yourself instead.

'I never seem to have time for myself'

It is natural that there is always something more to do. Find some time, and you can guarantee that it will immediately be filled. But this is an unhealthy situation. If you never have time for yourself, your natural ability to rejuvenate eventually begins to fail and you have less and less energy, will and drive, so that the tasks of everyday life take longer and longer to complete. Meditation reverses this process and has an effect similar to taking a holiday, helping you to recharge your batteries. If you never have time for yourself, then from a purely practical point of view it is important that you make some. My comments on the next statement may help you to do this.

'I want to meditate but it would be too time-consuming'

If this is why you have difficulty getting into meditation or committing yourself to it, let me unburden you. It simply isn't true. The effectiveness of meditation has no direct relationship with the amount of time spent doing it. You *can* spend a lot of time meditating to good effect, but equally there is no reason why you should. Later in this chapter I include an effective short meditation which can, believe it or not, occupy you for only a few seconds (Capturing the Moment, page 45). Length of time and quality of results are not dependent on one another.

An image which colours our attitude to meditation is that of the Buddhist monk who devotes his whole life to the practice. Banish this image from your mind. If such a lifestyle draws you, go for it, but my concern here is for using meditation in a way which enhances the quality of a Western lifestyle and is not an alternative to it.

'I would like to meditate, but there are always distractions'

The problem here is not one of time but of 'space', that is, having a suitable environment at your disposal. This is not easy if, for instance, you have a young family – try telling a three-year-old not to interrupt you for ten minutes!

An atmosphere conducive to meditation is certainly helpful, particularly if there are no noisy distractions or interruptions. However, this is making the false assumption that meditation is something separate from everyday life – that it can only be practised when everyday activity has ceased. In fact some meditations can be done within the context of normal daily activity; and, more importantly, the meditation experience should be carried over from a meditation session into everyday life. It is wrong to compartmentalise your meditation and regard it as something which only occurs under certain conditions. The whole point is that it can be integrated into your normal lifestyle. Its benefits can then be experienced not only while you are actually meditating but at all other times too. Quite literally the whole of life can become a meditative experience, one in which our self-awareness and effectiveness at conducting our lives are enhanced.

'I am very active, and meditation would be boring for me'

So you think that meditation means you are doing nothing, and with an empty mind too? The technique that I have developed owes much to insights into the workings of the mind offered by oriental meditation techniques but I have adapted them to suit the active mind which is constantly full of things to think, feel and do. Far from being boring, you will find that the opposite is true. Meditation in this context does not necessarily mean pushing thoughts and feelings to one side. You will discover that your imagination in particular is stimulated and encouraged and that the end result is new life and increasing enthusiasm, offering you the gift of discovering new dimensions to your existence. If you want to enjoy a combination of stimulation and relaxation, forget the idea that meditation is boring. You are on the verge of finding new worlds within you, an inner journey on which you are the explorer discovering uncharted territories and unlimited possibilities.

If you are a creative person, you will find meditation a practical means for stimulating your imagination, crystallising ideas and providing inspiration. Meditation offers the possibility of 'peak experiences', to use the term employed by humanistic psychologist Abraham Maslow (see page 236). He suggested that the experiences of the mystic, the genius, the inventor and the artist were commonly regarded as something at best unusual and at worst abnormal. He believed that this is not the right attitude, for, given the right encouragement, we all have the potential for such peak, life-enhancing experiences. Flashes of inspiration, the mystical feeling created spontaneously and unbidden at certain times of our lives, can be achieved through meditation. They cannot be turned on like a tap, but our awareness and experience of them can be greatly increased by opening up to the inspirational experiences that lie within us.

'The demands put on me by other people mean that I can't find the time or space to meditate. There always seem to be more important things to do.'

I have partly answered this challenge in the paragraphs above, but I want to add something here which I feel may be important for many readers. While we are growing up, demands are put on our behaviour from an early age. We are taught how to behave and how to become responsible adults, able to live in and contribute to society. Later on, work, career and family commitments make further demands on our time, behaviour, attitudes and beliefs. Any contact with the inner world of childhood and the dreams and aspirations that we may have had as a teenager or young adult are gradually lost or buried in the maelstrom of everyday life.

There comes a time when the demands placed on us by the outer world may lose their attraction, become dulled, perhaps repetitive and without any sense of meaning. By that time it is distinctly possible that the neglect of your inner life will have had a negative effect on your outer life circumstances – career, relationships, even health. The call comes to shift your attention inwards, so that you can listen again to the voice inside which speaks the truth when it tells you what *you* need. This means getting in touch, perhaps again, with your unlived, unfulfilled dreams and fantasies. Whether or not you achieve this through meditation – and meditation is certainly one route to take – without some appropriate action your inner life will eventually stagnate as you lose touch with your own needs as an individual. The result will be further deterioration of your outer circumstances.

I shall say more about this process of shifting the emphasis of awareness inwards to renew the source of your energy and life when I introduce the Mountain Journey on page 50. For now, in answer to the challenge that 'There are more important things to do', I am suggesting that priorities must eventually include one's inner life and needs, otherwise life itself stagnates and becomes meaningless. Everyone must make some time and space to rejuvenate. In that time and space, meditation is an excellent way to recharge your batteries.

'Meditation would help me to unwind, but by the end of the day I'm so tired all I want is to put my feet up and watch TV.'

This sort of inertia is difficult to combat – I've experienced it frequently myself. Many different things can be used as objects for meditation. The usual items include candles, crystals and flowers, so my next suggestion may seem bizarre. A television programme, too, can become an object for meditation! Using the method described on page 44, you can actually include the TV in your meditation.

The technique should lead you on and beyond your inertia so that the meditation will truly help you to relax and unwind. As you achieve this state you will begin to meditate more deeply and the day's stresses will simply ease and vanish. Perhaps through visualisation (page 226) you could even picture, using your imagination, an inner TV screen and meditate on the programmes that play themselves out on it.

Positive Thinking

Continuing with the theme of turning your awareness inwards, the key that opens the lock of the meditation experience is to become an observer of oneself, as in the first meditation in Chapter 1 (page 8). Try this one again. Close your eyes and become aware, in turn, of your thoughts, then your feelings, then the messages that your body is sending to you.

Doing this helps busy, pressured people because you will grow aware of messages from yourself, from your mind, emotions and body, which otherwise fail to get through to you because they are lost in the clutter of everyday activity, sounds, sensations and movement. Just stop for a moment and let them come through. Self-observation like this helps you to slip into — and then out from — the meditation experience.

There is a Zen meditation called Just Sitting, which is, in essence, the process that I have just described. To help you become inwardly still and calm the flow of thoughts, feelings and sensations, traditional meditation techniques introduce an object for meditation. One such 'object' can be a word or sound, a mantra, which you repeat in your mind or out loud so that your attention is continuously focused on it.

Human beings are suggestible — put a thought in our minds and we will respond to it. The principle of positive thinking has developed from this. If we are suggestible, then why not put positive thoughts in place? Link this with the use of a mantra and you have a tool which can be used to achieve any desired goal.

Set yourself a goal now. Do you want to lose weight, or become more confident, or simply more relaxed? In Transcendental Meditation, or TM, you are given a mantra, but in my technique you can choose your own. Your word might be 'Success', 'Confidence', or 'Tranquillity', applied to the above situations. You could choose a short phrase if you like, such as 'Calm and Tranquil', or you could use one of the positive affirmations given below.

AFFIRMATIONS

Life is beautiful. I am beautiful.

My inner strength is growing all the time.

My expectations will be fulfilled.

There are no limits in life.

MEDITATION FOR EVERY DAY

The universal life force fills me.

Infinite riches lie within me.

I am in control.

I accept responsibility for my life.

I open myself to strength and power.

I feel secure.

Life flows freely through me.

Abundance is here and now.

My needs are being met.

I have the courage to succeed.

I will achieve my aim.

My confidence is growing all the time.

I open myself to love.

I accept my whole self.

Life flows through me and I go with the flow.

Inner calm is mine.

I am free.

I accept all that comes to me.

I can transform my life.

The present moment is all that exists for me.

I open myself to receive life's bounty.

I am at the right place, at the right time.

Choose your affirmation to use as a mantra and we will incorporate it in a Positive Thinking meditation. You could also create your own affirmation, or adapt one of those given above to suit your own particular needs.

POSITIVE THINKING
10 minutes

Go through the following sequence:
— Body Relaxed technique (page 5).

— Self-observation (page 8).

— Counting Breaths (page 10).

— Now keep focused on your breathing but stop counting. Each time you breathe out say your mantra, either to yourself or out loud.

— Pause.

— Become aware of your breathing again. Breathe a little deeper. Become aware of your body and the room in which you are meditating, and when you are ready open your eyes.

The length of time that you spend on each part of the meditation is up to you — whatever you feel comfortable with. In Chapter 8 you will find a selection of short passages which are suitable subjects for meditation. Some of them can be used as mantras. Simply choose the mantra which you are drawn to and memorise it. Then use it in the meditation above.

Using a mantra as a tool for positive thinking can have direct benefits in many situations, particularly if you need to build confidence to succeed at a particular task or to achieve a goal. It is also an antidote to negative thinking, combatting the 'I can't' state of mind.

The traditional use of a mantra is to focus the mind so that distracting thoughts and feelings are not allowed to interfere with achieving a meditative state. A mantra can indeed help to achieve this state and will also induce the relaxation response described in Chapter 1. Any object can be used which helps to focus your attention and bring you into a state of relaxed heightened awareness. As mentioned earlier, a candle, a crystal, a flower or even a television set can be employed, either as an external object on which to focus your eyes, or as an inner visualised object of the imagination.

It is a helpful and encouraging exercise which you will find useful. However, I feel that most readers will be interested in developing more 'active' meditation experience in the sense of observing growth, change, movement, thoughts, images and feelings within themselves.

There is a simple meditation which, particularly for busy, over-stressed people, effectively calls forth the relaxation response and the meditation experience which follows from it. It can be achieved in a matter of seconds and is therefore a wonderful meditation if you are short of time. Needless to say, the experience can be extended for as long as you like.

In our normal waking consciousness we are bombarded by sensory experiences, pushed around by half-unconscious inner commands and demands. Our attention span and the objects of our attention are usually so short-lived that, instead of alighting on a particular piece of input information, we simply scan over it and move on to the next object that demands our attention.

To take just one source of information, our eyes are constantly receiving information about shape, colour, light

and shade so that our visual attention flits around like a
butterfly. So too with our other senses. We are so bombarded
by information that we may only notice something when it
suddenly disappears, like becoming aware of a clock when it
stops ticking.

Try this:

CAPTURING THE MOMENT
I minute

Relax . . . then direct your attention to a particular single visual
object or single sound and keep your attention on it for as
long as you can. If your attention wanders, bring it back. Allow
yourself to develop a heightened awareness of the object or
sound, particularly of its colour, texture or timbre.

You will find the experience of this simple act quite remarka-
ble. First, you will realise how mobile our attention usually is.
Secondly, you will discover that by letting your attention rest
for a while you invoke a state of relaxation and inner peace.
Thirdly, you will find that if you practise 'Capturing the
Moment' regularly you will develop a heightened sensitivity
and awareness of colour and sound. As a result you will
become more discriminating and able to surround yourself
with the sort of things that you feel good about and which
have a positive influence on you.

Creating an Inner Landscape

If you are serious about committing yourself to the inner
journey, then creating an appropriate inner environment within
which to work is a priority. In just the same way that I described
in Chapter 1 the external conditions and environment that are

conducive to meditation, it is important to create a corresponding inner environment, an inner workspace. This is the purpose of the next meditation. I shall ask you to visualise yourself in a garden, which you will then explore and get to know. The garden is an archetypal image of a protected, sacred piece of ground and crops up frequently in religious texts, in the alchemical tradition (see page 235) and in stories describing the initiate's search for understanding.

The meditation is one that you will be able to return to whenever you feel in need of working through something, perhaps a personal problem or a decision that has you in two minds. We will also use it for meditations later. The garden is a place of contemplation where you can seek inwardly for advice and inspiration. It is also an inner place where you can go to be alone with yourself, to give yourself time and space.

THE GARDEN
20 minutes

– Relaxation sequence (page 25).

– When you are ready, imagine that you are in a garden. It is not a garden that you know in your everyday world, but one which you create with your imagination, in your mind's eye. The garden is enclosed, perhaps by a wall, hedge or fence. . . . Build up in your mind a picture of the garden and yourself actually in it.

– Pause.

– Really be there, feeling the ground beneath your feet and the air or breeze against your face.

– Pause.

— What is the weather like? Is it a cloudy or a fine day? Is it co.
or warm? Is it a windy or a still day?

— Pause.

— What time of year is it? Is the garden growing through
spring, summer, autumn or winter?

— Pause.

— As you look around, does it seems to be a small or a large
garden? And what sort of condition is it in? Is it well kept, or is
it in need of attention?

— Pause.

— Know that this is your inner garden. It is an inner space
where you can go in your meditations at any time you wish. It
is a safe place where nothing and no one may go unless you
want them to enter. It is a place where you can go to resolve
any problems in your life ... a space for private contemplation.

— Pause.

— Begin to explore the garden. Really be there. What plants
and shrubs can you find? What flowers can you discover?
Look at them. Touch them. Respond to their beauty.

— Pause.

— Are there any birds or animals in the garden? They are your
friends and will not be frightened of you.

— Pause.

— Walk around the garden, exploring it and remembering

everything that you see, so that you might return again in the future.

— Pause.

— Now I want you to find one place in the garden that has a special atmosphere for you. An area that you feel drawn to and that can become your favourite place in the garden.

— Pause.

— What is it that draws you to this particular place? What do you experience there?

— Pause.

— While you are in this place, imagine that a friendly bird or animal comes to see you and talk with you. Accept whatever comes to you first.

— Pause.

— What does this creature wish to communicate to you? Listen to it.

— Pause.

— What does this creature need from you? Imagine that you are presented with a gift. Something that you can take with you and use in your everyday life. Accept whatever occurs to you first. Perhaps the friendly animal or bird will explain the meaning of this gift and how you can benefit from it.

— Pause.

— When you are ready, let the animal or bird disappear and contemplate for a moment what has just been happening.

— Pause.

— Now spend some more time enjoying being in the garden.

— Pause.

— Before you finish the meditation, breathe slightly more deeply, than you would normally.

— Pause.

— Become aware of your body and your surroundings, the place in which you are meditating.

— Pause.

— Stay completely relaxed and open your eyes. . . . Spend the next minute or two going over the meditation that you have just experienced.

— Pause.

— You can return to your inner garden any time that you wish to do so.

Reviewing Your Life

The next meditation gives you an opportunity to review your life, to contemplate where you have come from and where you are going. You will find yourself meditating on a mountain top, from where you can survey the panorama below. You have the opportunity to confront yourself — alone on the mountain you can discover yourself, who you are and where you are going in life. This is the same experience that 'real' explorers have.

The mountain is an image for those seeking enlightenment about themselves and self-knowledge. In *Zen and the Art of Climbing Mountains* Neville Schulman says:

> Mountains have always been magical and special places, often illustrated as mistily shrouded and portrayed as full of extreme mysteries. The gods lived on them; many kings built their castles and fortresses there; the ordinary people were usually forbidden access to them. Even to this day there is still one called Machapuchhare (the Fishtail), the sacred mountain of Nepal, which no one is permitted to climb.... Throughout the centuries mountains have exerted powerful influences on our imaginations, and, rightly so, many countries treat their own mountains as unique national treasures. A Hindu text from the *Devistrotra* states that 'So long as this land will have mountains and forests, so long will this earth survive.'

Experiences on the mountain can lead to a process of personal change and transformation. You may not return with the Ten Commandments, but you may discover an impulse or imperative that focuses your future life in a new direction or at least makes you aware of where you are going and where you want to go.

THE MOUNTAIN JOURNEY
25 minutes

— Relaxation sequence (page 25).

— When you are ready, imagine that you are in a field at the foot of a mountain. Stay in the field for a while, building up a picture of everything that you can see around you. Feel the ground under your feet and the air against your face. Really be there.

– Pause.

– What time of year is it? What is the weather like? What can you see?

– Pause.

– When you are ready, turn your attention to the mountain. Find the beginning of the path that will take you to the top, and slowly start to walk up it.

– Pause.

– Don't rush, but advance slowly and steadily up the mountain path. Enjoy the walk. What is the terrain like? Is it an easy or difficult climb?

– Pause.

– Breathe freely. The mountain air is pure and brings you fresh energy, cleansing your whole being.

– Pause.

– Spend the next few moments continuing to ascend the mountain path. Accept whatever experiences come to you. Accept whatever thoughts and feelings come to you. Enjoy this peaceful walk.

– Pause.

– You are now about halfway up the mountain, where you discover a spring of fresh water and a pool in the rocks. Touch the water and sprinkle a few drops on your face. Feel how cool and soothing the water is. You can drink some if you like.

– Pause.

– Let the pool become still. Then look into it. Look at your reflection. Observe carefully what you see.

– Pause.

– When you are ready and refreshed, continue your journey up the mountain path.

– Pause.

– What is the terrain like now? Is it changing as you get near the top of the mountain?

– Pause.

– Continue the climb until finally you reach the peak of the mountain.

– Pause.

– Find a place to sit or stand from where you can observe the panoramic view below you. What a beautiful sight meets your eyes.

– Pause.

– In life there is a mountain to climb. The view that you see from the top is a view of the panorama of life and all its experiences, laid out now in front of you.

– Pause.

– Begin to meditate on the panorama of your life. Imagine that you close your eyes on the mountain and begin to meditate. Allow thoughts and feelings about your life to rise up in you. Accept whatever comes.

– Pause (longer).

– Is there anything in your life that you need to change?

– Pause.

– Is there anything that you would like to achieve in the future?

– Pause.

– Is there anything in your past that is holding you back?

– Pause.

– When you have meditated on these aspects of your life and the changes – if any – that you would like to make, you will end your quiet time on the mountain top. But before you begin the descent, enjoy being where you are for a few moments more.

– Pause.

– Then, when you are ready, begin to walk back down the mountain path, going slowly and carefully.

– Pause.

– Eventually, you arrive again at the spring and the rock pool. Look again into the water and imagine that you see in it a symbol or picture that represents your need in life. Accept whatever you see. Allow it to become clearer and more real. This image represents your need in achieving your future aims in life. If you cannot visualise a symbol or image, try to capture a particular thought which indicates your need in life. Simply remember the image or the thought.

– Pause.

– Continue the descent down the mountain.

— Pause.

— Eventually you arrive again at the place from which you started. Look around . . . look back up the route that you have travelled. . . .

— Pause.

— Become aware of your breathing. . . . Breathe a little more deeply than you would normally. . . . Become aware of your body and physical surroundings. And when you are ready, open your eyes.

— Pause.

— While remaining completely relaxed, and before returning to your everyday activities, spend a little time remembering the experience of your Mountain Journey. In particular, remember the symbol, image or thought which represents your need in achieving your goal for the future.

— Pause.

— You can make the Mountain Journey again at any time you choose.

Inner Tuition

Meditation is about listening to yourself. There are no rules or regulations, except that if it feels right, then fine, and if not, then don't do it. Discovering whether something feels right or not is partly a matter of intuition, of following your own good advice and of being in contact with your natural wisdom. Being in touch with this source will give you psychological strength and confidence.

In the next meditation you will personify this aspect of yourself, and I shall ask you to visualise a wise person who embodies your own intuitions and wisdom and who has only your best interests at heart. The wise person, guide or teacher (even guru) is an important image or symbol that many people seek in their outer lives. The priest, mystic or guru fills this role and accepts the projection of the individual's unconscious on to them. But meditation means that you have no need to seek this teacher on an outer level. Some people travel great distances to find answers to the deeper questions about life, only to be directed by their teacher to look inward for enlightenment. The next meditation will put you in touch with a form of guidance that is not dependent on outer factors or on what others tell you you should or should not do, what you should and should not believe. First try the meditation and then read the following section, in which I say more about the importance of directing your attention inwards to discover what it is that you need in order to open up new dimensions to life.

Before you begin the meditation, just stop for a moment and choose one or two questions that you would like to ask an all-knowing, wise person – questions which are relevant to your own life at this time.

THE WISE PERSON
20 minutes

– Relaxation sequence (page 25).

– The Garden meditation (page 46).

– Imagine that you are in the garden and drawn to the special place that you found earlier. As you approach this place you see that there is someone already there waiting for you. You realise that this is a very wise person, someone who knows much about you and has come to guide and assist you.

– Pause.

– Allow the image of the wise person to become clearer so that you can see what he or she looks like. Take whatever comes to you.

– Pause.

– What is the wise person wearing? How old are they? How is the wise person responding to you, and how are you reacting to them?

– Pause.

– Approach the wise person and greet them. Does he or she have anything to say to you?

– Pause.

– Spend some time getting to know one another. You could ask what he or she is called. Ask where they have come from.

– Pause.

– Ask the wise person the questions that you wanted to ask, and let the response come to you.

– Pause.

– Is there anything else you would like to ask or discuss?

– Pause.

– Ask the wise person to make you a gift that will help you to stay in contact with your inner wisdom. Accept whatever comes to you first, and ask the wise person to explain the meaning of the gift and how you might use it.

— Pause.

— Thank him or her for being with you and allow the image of the person to fade so that you are alone again in the garden.

— Pause.

— Contemplate the experience that you have just had.

— Pause.

— When you are ready, let the image of the garden fade too and return your consciousness to your breathing, your body and the place in which you are meditating. Then open your eyes.

By the time we become adults, much of the experience of childhood has been lost. We start life full of vivid imaginations and, later, fantasies and dreams about how life *ought* to be and what it is going to be like for us in the future. We have dreams, perhaps of becoming rich or famous – or both! It is the exception when such a dream comes true. For most of us at some stage our illusions are shattered, or seem to become impossible as the demands and rigours of daily life leave their mark.

During this process of growing up, our personalities are maturing. Our attention is largely directed towards the outside world from where we receive impressions and facts about the nature of reality. The process starts very early in life – parents, then schoolteachers, then the experience of working life and creating our own family are all a part of growing up.

During this time an axis is developed which joins our

selves, our ego personalities and our self-awareness to the outside world.

INDIVIDUAL
AWARENESS ◄─────── **AXIS** ───────► **OUTSIDE**
'EGO' **WORLD**

The individual is, however, part of a much greater inner whole which includes our unconscious self as well as the conscious ego.

The unconscious is a store of information: some of it we can recall, while some is not so easy to get in touch with. All the things that we have ever learnt and experienced make up the unconscious. We are driven, usually without being aware of it, by its impulses and patterns of behaviour that we have built up over the years. Ways of being, thinking and reacting that seem natural to us are constructed from our experience of life. The unconscious is like another self, an inner self which has a great role to play in our total psychological make-up.

While we are directing our awareness and attention along the axis between 'individual self' and 'outside world', this inner self of the unconscious is being ignored. Eventually, if its needs are not met, it will begin to respond negatively.

The unconscious is our source of life. All our thoughts, feelings and imaginations, our will and conscious energy arise out of it and are sustained by it. Therefore, when the unconscious begins to respond in a negative sense, the result, in its extreme, is that our lives simply fall apart. Relationships go wrong, accidents happen, our careers stagnate, our energy levels are low and even our physical health can suffer. The unconscious is demanding attention. It can happen at any time, but is often characterised by the mid-life crisis, when our inner self has become sick and tired of being taken for granted, ignored or abused, as we live life only along the 'individual'/'outside world' axis. The time comes when we must shift our attention to a new axis, one which runs from our ego self-awareness to the inner world of the unconscious.

INNER SELF 'THE UNCONSCIOUS'	← AXIS →	INDIVIDUAL EGO AWARENESS

One way to change to this new axis is through meditation. By moving your attention inwards, you can begin to listen to the voice of inner wisdom and intuition. Little by little you will uncover those lost dreams, ideals and aspirations. To rejuvenate your life you can then begin to free them and express them. You will surprise yourself.

In *The Middle Passage* James Hollis describes the process like this:

In the first identity, childhood, the operative axis is the parent–child relationship. In the first adulthood the axis lies between ego and world. The ego, one's conscious being, struggles to project itself into the world and create a world within the world. Childhood dependency has been driven into the unconscious and/or projected onto various roles, and one is primarily oriented to the outer world. In the second adulthood . . . the axis connects ego and Self. It is natural for consciousness to assume that it knows all and is running the show. When its hegemony is overthrown, the humbled ego then begins the dialogue with the Self.

And again:

. . . one only needs the courage and the daily discipline to 'listen in'. . . . When we can internalize our dialogue while maintaining our contacts with the outer world, we then experience that linkage with the world of the soul previously provided by the ancient myths and religions.

I am not suggesting that you should cut yourself off from the outside world, as indeed James Hollis suggests in the above passage. The 'individual'/'outside world' axis must still play a role, but not to the detriment or exclusion of the 'inner self'/'individual' axis. You will discover that, by changing the emphasis to this new axis, rather than withdrawing from life the opposite will occur. You will become rejuvenated, and discover new passions and talents. Life will become full of purpose and meaning. Your health, energy and well-being will improve as your life becomes whole and fulfilled. Even your motives for living may change. Rather than performing your daily activities for a purely practical, materialistic motive of gain, you will do them simply out of the joy of living and the awareness of new dimensions to life, discovered first within yourself and then in the outside world too. The shifting from an outer to an inner axis can be a spiritually uplifting, even enlightening experience.

If you recognise the effects of a rebellious inner self, an unlived part of yourself which is seeking to be heard, constant relationship/work/health/career/money/family problems, loss of energy and a sense of the futility of life, turn inwards to discover the life that you are missing. The Wise Person meditation is the key to this discovery.

Interpreting Symbols

In the meditations in which I have asked you to use your imagination and picture certain images – a garden, a mountain, and so on – you are experiencing a 'guided meditation' and entering into the realm of symbols which are all pregnant with meaning and future possibilities.

The unconscious communicates through thoughts, feelings and images, which are symbolic in nature. When you experience a guided meditation, the images that come to you are rather like dreams, except that you can direct them towards a particular purpose, or have a particular goal in mind as you set off on one of these meditations. Once you have set the scene, allow your unconscious to do all the work and accept whatever it may present to you.

When you have finished a guided meditation you will naturally want to find out what the symbols represent. The process is similar to dream interpretation. In the first instance, it is best not to jump to conclusions but to let the meaning unfold naturally. Coincidences and experiences in your everyday life will tend to synchronise in some way with your meditations, helping your insight and understanding to grow. This should be a natural process.

You may find a *dictionary of symbols* useful, which describes the traditional, archetypal meaning of symbols. For example, a snake or serpent is a symbol of wisdom; birds and animals in particular have their own associated symbolic meanings. A dictionary of this kind will help to amplify the meaning of your guided meditation experiences, but beware. First, you may find it annoying that, no matter how comprehensive the dictionary, your unconscious will almost inevitably produce a symbol that isn't in it. Secondly, and more importantly, the dictionary will give only a particular and archetypal meaning, such as serpent = wisdom. It will not say what a particular image may mean to you and this is just as important to its interpretation. One person's wisdom may be another person's fear, or something not to be trusted at all.

You may find it useful to keep a *diary* recording your meditation experiences (see page 229). The memory of them can fade quite quickly – again there is a similarity with dreams – and you may only see the relevance of a particular meditation at a later date. Also, you will be interested to discover the pattern of development in your meditations over a period of time. As you write them down you will find yourself making associations, amplifying their meaning and discovering more about their significance for you.

I will end this chapter with another guided meditation, called the Inner Temple. You will face three doors, one marked 'Past', one 'Present' and one 'Future'. You will have the opportunity to open each door in turn.

This is an extension of the idea behind the Mountain Journey, in that it will help you to see what has led you to your present circumstances and where they may lead you in the future. Don't forget that, if any questions have occurred to you by now, you will probably find them answered in Chapter 10.

THE INNER TEMPLE – PAST, PRESENT AND FUTURE
25 minutes

– Relaxation sequence (page 25).

– Imagine that you are inside a temple or sacred building of some sort – not one that you know in your outer life but one that exists inside you in your imagination. Build up a picture of yourself in the temple. Really be there – feel the ground under your feet and move around touching what you see.

– Pause.

– Sense the special peaceful atmosphere that exists here.

– Pause.

– There are seats in the temple and a focal point or altar from where services or ceremonies can be conducted.

62

Spend some time looking around and soaking up the atmosphere.

– Pause.

– Is this an old or a new place? Are there signs that it is used regularly or not?

– Pause.

– Go to the focal point or altar. Behind it you will find three doors in the temple wall. Go and stand in front of them.

– Pause.

– The door to your left is marked 'Past'. Imagine that you open this door and look through it. What can you see?

– Pause.

– If you wish, you can go through the door to explore, or simply stay where you are, observing what you can see and what unfolds before you.

– Pause.

– When you are ready, close the door and stand in front of the next door to the right of the first. This is marked 'Present'. Open this door and look through it. What can you see?

– Pause.

– If you wish, you can go through the door to explore, or simply stay where you are, observing what you can see and what unfolds before you.

– Pause.

– When you are ready, close the door and stand in front of the next door to the right of the second one. This is marked 'Future'. Open this door and look through it. What can you see?

– Pause.

– If you wish, you can go through the door to explore, or simply stay where you are, observing what you can see and what unfolds before you.

– Pause.

– When you are ready, stand in front of the three doors again. They are now all closed before you. Return to the main body of the temple and imagine that you kneel or sit in front of the altar or centrepiece.

– Pause.

– Contemplate the experiences that you have just had. Recall them and meditate on them.

– Pause.

– You can return to this place at any time you wish in the future – perhaps you could meet a guide or your wise person here, who will help explain the meaning of the temple and its doors and show you what you should do.

– Pause.

– For now, let the image of the temple fade and return your awareness to your breathing. Breathe a little more deeply than normal. Become aware of your body and the place in which you are meditating. When you are ready, stay completely relaxed and open your eyes.

Now that I have covered the basics of meditation and introduced some possibilities for further exploration, we can turn to some specific applications. In Chapter 3 I will introduce some colour meditations and describe their associations with the 'chakras' or different centres of awareness in the body.

3

COLOUR
MEDITATIONS

We tend to think of the centre of our self-awareness as being in the head, where we experience thinking, but there are other centres of awareness in the body. For example, emotions tend to well up from the area between the chest and lower stomach. Throughout history, different organs have been credited as being the seat of our consciousness; the heart and liver were the most notable ones.

Sexual drives stem from the lower part of the body and, although it is not so easy to perceive, the centre from which our will operates is seated in this area too. This centre is more difficult to describe as a centre of awareness because the source of our will is largely unconscious. However, it can be described as emanating from the lower part of the body, and it is possible to see how this can be by associating sexual drive with the will. Sexual impulses and instincts are a great driving force in life, and the energy that derives from them can be directed into almost every human activity. The centres of thinking, feeling and willing are correspondingly associated with the upper, middle and lower parts of the body.

If you have read about philosopher Rudolf Steiner's 'anthroposophy' you will recognise this threefold division of

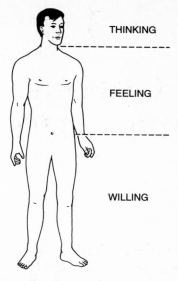

THINKING

FEELING

WILLING

The centres of our thinking, feeling and willing are associated with the upper, middle and lower parts of the body respectively.

our natures, for he placed great emphasis on it as a means for understanding the subtle anatomy of the human being.

Another way of describing this subtle anatomy of the centres of consciousness is by the *chakras*, a term from an ancient Eastern language, Sanskrit. The chakras can be understood as an extension of this idea of parts of the body which seem to be the centres for different types of consciousness or awareness. Instead of three centres of awareness, seven chakras are usually described, each one representing a different way in which we experience ourselves.

More about the chakras can be found in the ancient Hindu religious texts called *The Upanishads*, which indicate their locations and provide symbolic descriptions of each one. Pictures, images, animals, birds, gods and goddesses are used to describe their qualities and properties in both an intellectual and a symbolic fashion, giving a 'feel' for what the chakras are all about. The descriptions which follow include some of the associations, or *correspondences* (see page 230), made with the chakras to amplify their meaning and significance.

Correspondences with the chakras include different *colours*. The correspondences indicated in the following paragraphs are not given in the original Hindu texts but were probably added after the system of chakras was introduced into the West. If you would like to learn about the chakras, an excellent introduction is given by Naomi Ozaniec in *The Elements of the Chakras*.

For our purposes, the association that I want to use for meditation is the correspondence of each rainbow colour with the seven chakras.

We respond immediately to different colours liking particular ones and their hues and combinations, and disliking others. There is also a psychological basis for our response to colour: the red end of the spectrum tends to be stimulating,

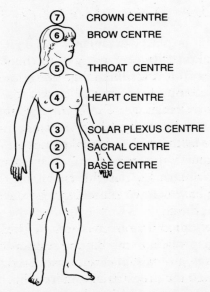

The seven chakras represent seven different centres of awareness.

while the blue end is calming. Different colours have different symbolic significance. Red, for example, can in different circumstances represent love or anger, green can represent new life, yellow is the colour of the intellect, and so on. Meditating on a particular colour can create a particular effect, and knowing the associations with a colour means that it is possible to use colour in meditation to achieve an expanded awareness of a particular aspect of our being – a particular chakra, or centre of awareness. (The specific healing properties of the various colours are explained in the chapter on healing: see page 111.)

The chakras are particularly useful in amplifying the correspondences that are made with each colour. You could try all the following colour meditations or select one or two to which you feel intuitively drawn. The numbers that appear after each chakra heading refer to their position on the chakras diagram.

The Base Centre (1)

The base chakra or *muladhara* (derived from the Sanskrit *mula*, meaning root, and *adhara*, meaning base or support) is located at the base of the spine, between the anus and the genitals. Its function is associated with grounding, with the will to survive and stability. Its physical associations are with the sense of smell, with the adrenal glands and with the legs, feet, bones and large intestine. It is associated with the element of Earth, which is the element of stability and security. The base centre's animal symbols are the bull, the elephant and the ox.

This centre represents our instincts and basic drives. The adrenal glands associated with it are responsible for what is known as the 'fight or flight' response to confrontation or danger, through the production of adrenalin.

The colour associated with the base chakra is *red*, the

colour of raw energy, instinct, sex and the life force. It can heighten blood pressure and increase adrenalin levels. Red, as mentioned earlier, can represent the extremes of violent anger and love. It is a colour to use in meditation if you want to release or increase any of these qualities in yourself.

As with any of the colours, you may find that my suggested associations do not seem to work for you. You must therefore try the meditations with an attitude of openness; what is important is what you experience. Your personal associations and experiences are more important than the traditional correspondences, which provide a map but not the country.

Some colour associations for red are:

- dark red: passion, love
- reddish brown: sensuality
- crimson: desire

COLOUR RED
20 minutes

— Relaxation sequence (page 25).

— Picture in your mind's eye a red flower floating in a bowl of water.

— Pause.

— Look at the flower and take it in your hands.

— Pause.

— Examine carefully the different formations of the petals.

— Pause.

— Notice all the different shades of red that are present in the petals.

– Pause.

– Find out if the flower has a scent. Imagine that you smell the flower.

– Pause.

– Place the flower back in the bowl of water and meditate again on its colour.

– Pause.

– Let the colour grow in intensity until you can sense its vibrations in every part of your body.

– Pause.

– Imagine that you are breathing the colour red.

– Pause.

– Fill yourself with colour and feel how it makes you warm and alive.

– Pause.

– Direct the colour into your base chakra.

– Pause.

– Allow any thoughts, feelings or sensations in response to the colour red arise in you. Allow them to come and to grow. Observe them and the effect that they have on you.

– Pause.

– Allow the colour to die down again until you see in front of you once more the bowl of water on which floats the red flower.

– Pause.

– Contemplate the experience that you have just had.

– Pause.

– Breathe slightly more deeply and become aware of your body and the place in which you are meditating.

– Pause.

– Stay completely relaxed and open your eyes.

The Sacral Centre (2)

The sacral chakra or *svadisthana* is positioned near the base centre and within the abdomen, midway between the genitals and the navel. Its function is to do with pleasure, sexuality and procreation. It is also associated with the cleansing of the body via the excretory processes. The Sanskrit name is said to mean 'one's own abode' or 'sweetness', although there is some debate about this. Its physical associations are with the womb, kidneys, reproductive and circulation systems and bladder. An association is made also with the sense of taste and the glands of the ovaries and testicles. Its associated element is Water, which is the element of feelings and emotional instincts. The animal symbols of this centre include all the creatures that live in the sea.

The sacral chakra is the seat of the creative urge, particularly in a sexually motivated sense – what I described in the introduction to this chapter as the will. The colour associated with this centre is *orange*; a colour of joy and happiness, it is an antidote to heaviness, sloth and depression. Orange will strengthen your will and self-confidence, although in excess the opposite may occur. Its positive benefits bring freedom to thoughts and feelings, so in meditation it is a good colour to use to open up the inner world and allow the unconscious to create freely the images and experiences that represent the source of creativity.

Some colour associations for orange are:
- bright, clear orange: health and vitality
- deep orange: pride
- muddy orange: muddled thinking

COLOUR ORANGE
20 minutes

— Relaxation sequence (page 25).

— Imagine tht you are holding an orange-coloured fruit. (Use a real one if you like).

— Pause.

— Examine the texture of the skin and be aware of how it feels against your skin.

— Pause.

— Peel the fruit and again examine its texture and the different shades of orange that it contains.

— Pause.

— Begin to eat the fruit and let its taste burst through your taste buds.

— Pause.

— Meditate on the colour orange.

— Pause.

– Let the colour grow in intensity until you can sense its vibrations in every part of your body.

– Pause.

– Imagine that you are breathing the colour orange.

– Pause.

– Fill yourself with the colour and feel how it brings you physical pleasure.

– Pause.

– Direct the colour into your sacral chakra.

– Pause.

– Allow any thoughts, feelings or sensations in response to the colour orange to arise in you. Allow them to come and to grow. Observe them and the effect that they have on you.

– Pause.

– Allow the colour to die down until you visualise the orange fruit again, which has been made whole, its skin still intact.

– Pause.

– Contemplate the experience that you have just had.

– Pause.

– Breathe slightly more deeply and become aware of your body and the place in which you are meditating.

– Pause.

– Stay completely relaxed and open your eyes.

The Solar Plexus Centre (3)

The solar plexus chakra or *manipura* is located in the spine at the level of the solar plexus. Its Sanskrit name means 'city of jewels' or 'lustrous gem'. Its element is Fire, which is the element of intuition and imagination. This centre is associated with the will and power, which are generated out of intense, 'burning' emotion. Its physical associations are with the digestive system, the liver and spleen. Its associated gland is the spleen, and the sense linked with this chakra is that of sight. The ram is an animal symbol of the solar plexus chakra. People who suffer from laziness, sluggishness, depression or digestive problems should concentrate on this centre, feeling heat and energy radiating from it.

The colour associated with this centre is *yellow*, a colour of the intellect and thought – yellow stimulates mental activity, encouraging clarity of thought and freedom from obsessional thoughts, feelings and habits. Yellow is also the colour of sunshine and the day, stimulating pleasure in oneself and heightening self-awareness.

Some colour associations for yellow are:

- golden yellow: clarity and awareness, expanded consciousness
- pale primrose yellow: steadfast purpose and inner strength, intellectual prowess, vision
- dull yellow: false optimism

COLOUR YELLOW
20 minutes

– Relaxation sequence (page 25).

— Imagine that you are lying on golden yellow sand, sunbathing.

— Pause.

— Feel warm and comfortable throughout your body as you absorb the sun's rays.

— Pause.

— Turn your attention to the sand. Pick some up and let it slowly slip through your fingers. Watch the sand fall from your grasp. Be aware of every detail.

— Pause.

— Look carefully at the grains.

— Pause.

— See in them different hues of yellow. Let the crystals reflect the yellow of the sun's rays.

— Pause.

— Meditate on the colour yellow.

— Pause.

— Let the colour grow in intensity until you can sense its vibrations in every part of your body.

— Pause.

— Imagine that you are breathing the colour yellow.

— Pause.

– Fill yourself with the colour and feel how it creates in you great clarity and heightened awareness, making you strong and confident.

– Pause.

– Direct the colour into your solar plexus chakra. Allow any thoughts, feelings or sensations in response to the colour yellow to arise in you. Allow them to come and to grow. Observe them and observe the effect that they have on you.

– Pause.

– Allow the colour to die down again until you return to bathing in the sunlight.

– Pause.

– Contemplate the experience you have just had.

– Pause.

– Breathe slightly more deeply and become aware of your body and the place in which you are meditating.

– Pause.

– Stay completely relaxed and open your eyes.

The Heart Centre (4)

The heart chakra or *anahata* is based between the fourth and fifth vertebrae at the level of the chest. Its Sanskrit name means 'unstruck' or 'unbeaten'. This is an allusion to a sound which has no beginning or source, which does not emanate from any struck note, and signifies the first centre of con-sciousness to bring an awareness of the infinite and the absolute. It marks the mid- or meeting-point between the lower chakras representing the physical world and the upper chakras of the spirit and conscious awareness. The heart centre's element is Air, the element of the rational mind, and it is associated with the function and experience of love. Its physical associations are with the lungs, heart, arms and hands and with the thymus gland. The sense linked with this chakra is touch and it has creature symbols of birds, the dove in particular, and the antelope.

At this point, the awareness and experience to be awoken are those of love and compassion. This does not just mean love in our personal relationships, but a more encompassing love for all things and for life itself. This love awakens compassion, which means a sensitivity towards, and even a sympathetic experience of, the plight of others.

Compassion means to feel for others and to respond supportively to this. From the sympathetic experience of compassion comes the ability to heal, and healing comes through the heart centre. It is no coincidence that the sense of touch is mentioned in association with this chakra, for it is through touch that our ability to heal others, with the awakening of the heart chakra, can reach out into the outside world.

The activation of this chakra brings increased sensitivty of touch, so that we can detect the energy fields of others and the imbalances that cause illness in the subtle and physical bodies. The ability to heal comes from the awakening of compassion and the ability to love, from the awakening of the heart centre.

The colour associated with this centre is *green*, the colour of nature and new life. This colour and the heart chakra are associated with harmony and balance, and indeed, as explained above, this centre is a meeting-point of balance between the higher and lower chakras.

Balance means a right relationship between functions

which can otherwise oppose one another or cancel one another out. This can apply to many things – relationships with other people, between the conscious self and the unconscious, between our inner selves and the outside world. To be healthy, these must be correctly balanced, in a right relationship that makes them whole or healed.

Some colour associations for green are:
- light green: prosperity and success
- mid-green: adaptability and versatility
- clear green: sympathy
- darkened or muddy green: deceit or self-delusion

COLOUR GREEN
20 minutes

– Relaxation sequence (page 25).

– Imagine that it is a warm summer's day and you are walking barefoot across a grassy field.

– Pause.

– You feel the cool, refreshing grass beneath the soles of your feet. Focus on the sensation.

– Look at the grass closely now and observe its texture and the different hues of green that can be found even in a single blade.

– Pause.

– Meditate on the colour green.

– Pause.

– Stand upright and imagine that you are meditating on the sensation of the grass beneath your feet. Then begin to absorb the vibrations of the colour green through your feet and up into your body.

— Pause.

— Let the colour grow in intensity until you can sense its healing vibrations in every part of your body.

— Pause.

— Direct the colour into your heart chakra.

— Pause.

— Allow any thoughts, feelings or sensations in response to the colour green to arise in you. Allow them to come and grow. Observe them and the effect that they have on you.

— Pause.

— Allow the colour to die down again until you feel the grass once more beneath your feet.

— Pause.

— Contemplate the experience that you have just had.

— Pause.

— Breathe slightly more deeply and become aware of your body and the place in which you are meditating.

— Pause.

— Stay completely relaxed and open your eyes.

The Throat Centre(5)

The throat centre or *vishudda* is located in the throat itself. Its Sanskrit name means 'to purify', and its function is to do with communication and creativity which stem from the awakening of the intuition, a state of inner knowing. The physical associations with the throat chakra are the neck and shoulders and the thyroid and parathyroid glands. It is linked with the sense of hearing.

When working at this seat of awareness you are activating the ability to become involved in the creative process in the sense that artists talk about being a channel, not a creator, of their work. The gift of speech is linked with this centre and its corresponding receptive sense of hearing. This does not simply mean the physical sense of hearing, but the ability to hear inwardly, to receive audible impressions in just the same way that inner images or visualisations can be created or channelled through from the unconscious.

The ability to channel creative impulses, whether music, prose, poetry or any other creative form, is brought to life with the awakening of this centre. It is also given the attribute of prophecy, the ability to be aware of the relationship between past, present and future.

The colour associated with this centre is *blue*, the colour of peace and tranquillity. It is associated with protection and also with infinity and the absolute. Blue is the colour of the teacher of life's secrets and hence its association with this centre's power to reveal past, present and future through developing intuition, or 'inner tuition'.

Some colour associations with blue are:
- clear blue: religious inspiration and feelings
- pale blue: devotion and inspiration
- bright blue: artistic creativity, intuition

COLOUR BLUE
20 minutes

— Relaxation sequence (page 25).

— Imagine that it is a clear day and that the sky is bright blue.

— Pause.

— Look into the sky and contemplate its depths.

— Pause.

— Imagine that the blue sky descends around you to become a beautiful, sumptuous cloak which enfolds you.

— Pause.

— What does it feel like to wear this blue mantle? Meditate on the colour blue.

— Pause.

— Let the intensity of the colour blue increase until you begin to absorb it through every pore in your body, even breathing in the colour blue.

— Pause.

— Direct the colour into your throat chakra.

— Pause.

— Allow any thoughts, feelings or sensations in response to the colour blue to arise in you. Allow them to come and to grow. Observe them and the effect that they have on you.

— Pause.

– In particular, listen inwardly and become aware of what it is that seeks expression through you. Simply listen.

– Pause.

– Allow the colour to die down and return your attention again to the blue cloak.

– Pause.

– Let the blue cloak become the infinite sky again.

– Pause.

– Contemplate the experience you have just had.

– Pause.

– Breathe slightly more deeply and become aware of your body and the place in which you are meditating.

– Pause.

– Stay competely relaxed and open your eyes.

The Brow Centre (6)

The brow chakra or *ajna* is located just above the bridge of the nose. Its Sanskrit name means 'to know', 'to perceive' or 'to command', giving clues to the significance of this centre. It has become associated with the concept of the third eye, meaning the possibility of a new sense which can be used to perceive beyond the range of the normal five senses. Its inner state is the developing of self-mastery, and the associated body parts are the eyes and the brain.

It is interesting that one Hindu deity associated with this chakra is Sakti Hakini, depicted as a figure whose right side is male and whose left side is female. Also, an image associated with the brow centre is of a flower with only two petals. This can be interpreted as representing the unity of the two ways in which we, as human beings, perceive our world, through either the left or right hemisphere of the brain (each being one petal of the flower). The left hemisphere functions through logic and rational thought and controls the right side of the body, the male side of the deity. The right hemisphere is in control of the left side of the body, depicted in the deity as female, and is the area of the brain that generates intuition and the imaginative faculties.

This chakra is a seat of awareness for the experience that the two petals of the flower together form a whole, each part having equal value. It is the area where we experience our thoughts and where visualisation takes place.

The colour associated with this centre is *indigo*, which is the colour of borderlands between the polar opposites. It can be understood as representing a curtain between the conscious and the unconscious self, and we shall use this image in the following meditation.

Some colour associations with indigo are:

● attainment, particularly in a spiritual sense, self-mastery, wisdom and saintliness.

COLOUR INDIGO
20 minutes

— Relaxation sequence (page 25).

— Imagine that you are painting a picture of a night-time scene. You are painting the night sky in a deep indigo. You add some stars and the moon to your picture.

— Pause.

— You finish the picture and then contemplate the night sky you have created.

— Pause.

— Let the colour indigo intensify until you move into it and it moves into you. Meditate on the colour indigo.

— Pause.

— Fill your mind and yourself with this colour, and then direct it into your brow centre.

— Pause.

— Allow any thoughts, feelings or sensations in response to the colour indigo to arise in you. Allow them to come and to grow. Observe them and the effect that they have on you.

— Pause.

— Now imagine that the indigo colour becomes a curtain or veil in front of you. Allow the curtain to draw back and become aware of what lies behind it.

— Pause.

— Spend some time looking behind the curtain. Accept whatever you find and allow it to change and develop.

— Pause.

— Draw the curtain back again and then let the image fade. Become aware again of the picture that you painted at the beginning.

— Pause.

– Contemplate the picture and the experience that you have just had.

– Pause.

– Breathe slightly more deeply and become aware of your body and the place in which you are meditating.

– Pause.

– Stay completely relaxed and open your eyes.

The Crown Centre (7)

The crown chakra or *sahasrara* is at the crown of the head. Its Sanskrit name means 'thousandfold', and the inner experience which the awakening of this centre brings is the state of bliss. The function of the crown centre is to create union between the conscious and the unconscious self, between the material and spiritual realms. The body parts with which it is associated are the brain, cerebral cortex and the whole of the body. The serpent awakened from its slumber is a symbol associated with the crown centre, and Shiva is its Hindu deity.

This is perhaps the most difficult chakra to describe, as its associations are with the mystical experience of union with the absolute. It is very rare to experience a peak experience, enlightenment, but just a few seconds once in their lifetime have been enough to inspire the great saints, philosophers, artists, scientists and religious leaders throughout history. The message is that, having once touched the state of 'bliss', you will never forget it. As a result your life may be changed for ever.

I am not suggesting that this condition can be arrived at by activation of the crown chakra through a simple meditation, but meditation will enable you to become aware of other possibilities, other dimensions operating in your life. Our normal consciousness is of separation between the polar opposites; in this book we are dealing in particular with the polar opposites of the conscious and unconscious selves, and the inner/outer realms of experience. The union that this chakra offers is the union of these opposites. When this marriage occurs, a third state of awareness arises, which can be represented by the symbol of a child. Giving birth to this new child within is perhaps a more appropriate Western symbol than the traditional oriental one of the risen serpent, but the significance is the same.

The colour associated with this centre is *violet*, the colour of pure consciousness and spiritual awakening. It also represents humility and is said to have great healing properties.

Some colour associations with violet are:
- deep violet: high spiritual attainment, transcendence
- pale violet: cosmic consciousness, union with the divine

COLOUR VIOLET
20 minutes

– Relaxation sequence (page 25).

– Imagine that you are holding a piece of amethyst which has a lovely violet hue (hold a real crystal if you like).

– Pause.

– Feel the texture of the crystal and look closely at its shape and form.

– Pause.

– Look at the colour of the crystal and note carefully the different shades and hues of violet that you can find in it.

– Pause.

– Let the crystal radiate its colour, which grows in intensity.

– Pause.

– Imagine that you absorb the colour into your body, breathing it in through every pore.

– Pause.

– Fill yourself with the colour violet, then direct it up through the top of your head and into the crown chakra.

– Pause.

– Visualise yourself as a perfect spiritual being. What does this mean to you?

– Pause.

– Accept any thoughts, feelings or images that arise in response to this. Allow them to come and to grow. Observe them and the effect that they have on you.

– Pause.

– Perhaps there is a part of your body which needs healing. Become aware of this and direct the violet colour into it. Feel the cleansing effect of the violet colour.

– Pause.

– Let the colour fade away now and become aware once more of the amethyst that you are holding.

– Pause.

– Contemplate the experience that you have just had.

– Pause.

– Breathe slightly more deeply and become aware of your body and the place in which you are meditating.

– Pause.

– Stay completely relaxed and open your eyes.

This completes the sequence of colour meditations associated with the chakras. In the last meditation I introduced the idea of healing using a combination of a crystal and its colour. We will explore this further in chapter 4. Before concluding this chapter, however, here is a meditation which can be used to activate any of the seven centres of awareness. The Sanskrit word 'chakra' means a wheel.

SPINNING THE WHEEL
15 minutes

– Before beginning, decide which chakra you would like to work on and note its associated colour.

– Relaxation sequence (page 25).

– Become aware of the part of your body where the chakra you have chosen to stimulate is situated. Imagine there a wheel that begins to turn.

– Pause.

– Let the wheel turn faster and faster, and as it turns it radiates the colour associated with this chakra.

– Pause.

– Let the colour grow in intensity until it is radiating out from you in all directions.

– Pause.

– Let the wheel slow and the colour fade until the wheel has stopped turning.

– Pause.

– Contemplate how you are feeling and watch any thoughts or images that arise in you.

– Pause.

– Breathe slightly more deeply, becoming aware of your body and the place in which you are meditating.

– Pause.

– Stay completely relaxed and open your eyes.

Don't forget that meditation should be an enjoyable experience. If you ever feel uncomfortable with a particular meditation, you will do no harm by bringing it to an end at any point simply by opening your eyes.

In the next chapter we will consider meditation as part of an overall healing strategy, applying the technique of positive thinking and developing the use of colour and crystals.

4

HEALING
MEDITATIONS

Meditation can become part of the healing process on whatever level is appropriate, ranging from dealing with the problems of everyday life to assisting the physical body in its hour of need.

Holistic Healing

Healing in a holistic sense, rather than being concerned simply with the problem itself, is concerned with the whole person. This is the description that is usually given of holistic healing, but what does it actually mean, and how can meditation be a part of this? We have already seen how meditation is the creation of relaxed awareness, and we have placed particular emphasis on becoming self-aware. This is an essential ingredient of holistic healing. Many illnesses and many difficulties in life have a direct relationship with the way we treat ourselves, often unconsciously, and with our attitudes. Becoming aware of the impulses that drive us is the first step to recognising that the solution to a problem might well lie within ourselves. Then we can take responsibility for developing a solution or cure.

As the meditation experience begins to grow, it is likely that many preconceived ideas fall away or change, and this is exactly what can happen to one's attitude to health and healing. As you become aware of certain relationships – between our conscious personality and the unconscious, between mind and body, between our inner attitudes and beliefs and the circumstances of the outer world – you will start to realise that healing is not simply a case of making better but of making whole, hence the emphasis on holistic healing. Both 'whole' and 'holistic' imply this attitude or process.

Polarities of Mind and Body

I am not suggesting that this is an alternative form of healing. What it can do is complement other forms of therapy by revealing those areas where you can help yourself by making changes in certain attitudes and areas of your life in order to create the right relationship between mind and body.

Indeed, in my experience the process involving the development of self-awareness through meditation can have the opposite effect – it seems to make matters worse before they get better! Without awareness that you have a problem you can sail through life blissfully unaware that anything is wrong, even though others might be suffering in your wake as a result of your attitudes and behaviour. Becoming aware of an inner problem can mean that you suddenly fall into a state of dis-ease with yourself. This is why matters get worse. However, this is ust part of the healing process, rather like a homoeopathic cure which makes you worse before you get better. Meditation brings self-awareness, and this can be described metaphorically as biting the apple of knowledge – remember how Adam suddenly became aware of himself, and there was then a price to pay? After this act, the Garden of Eden was out of bounds and the realities of life had to be faced.

You may recognise this scenario as your meditation develops. At first everything is wonderful; you are in the Garden of Eden, where you have discovered the solution to all your problems – you have found the secret of your life. Then you can go no further. Nothing seems to be happening. You relapse into your previous state, and it can be even worse than before.

This is a crisis point, at which you have to decide whether to find a completely different approach, or whether this moment is part of the natural process on the way to self-awareness and healing. I can't answer this question for you, but I can say that the situation happens over and over again.

What is happening is a process of developing a relationship with your inner self, with your unconscious. It is not unlike the progress of a marriage. First, you get to know the other person, then there is the marriage and honeymoon period in which everything is wonderful and exciting. After that things settle down and nothing else seems to be happening other than dealing with the mundane problems of everyday life, until suddenly matters take a turn for the worse and the question of divorce looms on the horizon. What do you do? See it through or get divorced?

There may be a genuine need to give up this particular relationship. But if you do, the chances are that in your next relationship you will go through the whole process again – and will go on repeating it until you become aware of what is going on inside you. The same applies to the inner relationship formed during meditation, and it is also an allegory for the healing process itself. The crunch is that, if you have a bad relationship with yourself, running away from it is, in the end, not possible.

When you meditate you are conducting a sort of alchemical experiment in which you are a flask containing all the constituent parts of your personality. When these are mixed, shaken and heated, the pressure can build up to become quite unbearable. In this experiment new substances – that is, new parts of yourself – are created. The alchemists used to say that all the work would be wasted if the sealed flask were to be broken open before the end of the experiment. In terms of meditation, breaking the flask is a way of saying 'I give up.'

So healing is not simply a case of making better. In fact there is a case to argue that some illnesses, whether of the physical body or in our life circumstances, are natural events – not to be destroyed, conquered or got rid of, but to be worked through so that they can lead us on to the next part of our lives. Constantly denying our problems by suppressing them or projecting them on to other people only means that they will rear up again later in a more deadly form.

If this makes sense to you and you can relate it to your own life circumstances, it is worth pursuing the point further. Healing, in the sense of making whole, suggests bringing conflicting areas of life together in a way that their relationship changes, so that instead of conflict there is mutual support. You can apply this principle to your opposite partner in the outside world, or to your opposite partner within you, the unconscious.

The aim is to seek a true marriage between the two polarities – not so that one dominates or takes over the life of the other, but so that each can have a valid contribution to make. For someone who is over-rational or materialistic in their attitude to life, this means developing their imagination and intuition. And, of course, the opposite applies to someone who is too caught up in their fantasies, or who does not think for themselves.

Through developing this right relationship with yourself your outer life circumstances will change too, and your outer relationships will begin to grow and mature. Meditation is far from being an act of doing nothing! Form a right relationship with yourself, and you will be healed. Form a right relationship with yourself, and your life will be healed. You can heal your life.

The physiological effects of meditation are well known – reduction of stress levels, blood pressure and so on. But these are in a sense by-products of the central effect of meditation, which is to act on the mind, both conscious and unconscious. This area is usually not stressed as being of practical benefit, but I would contest this and state the opposite, that to know oneself has a direct effect on all aspects of life from the physical to the spiritual. I must stress again, however, that taking this route does not mean that all the effects will be immediately positive. Meditation can lead to inner challenges and tests which must be faced and may not be easy.

Perhaps a glimpse of the Garden of Eden is not a bad thing, for it will leave a lasting memory and impression of what it is possible to achieve, a memory that you can hold with you as you travel your personal route through the inner life. Think of yourself as a pilgrim setting out on the road to find the Holy Grail. Remember that the Knights of the Round Table were shown a vision of the Grail which inspired them to set off on their adventures. And so they did, to meet with the challenges that confronted them as they travelled on their way. You could stay at home if you want to, but for me – and I hope for you too – the adventure of the inner pilgrimage is a beckoning call which should not be resisted.

Meditation as Part of a Healing Strategy

From the sublime now to the practical. Later in this chapter I will give you some healing meditations based on the principles of spiritual and crystal healing. Here first are some strategies for dealing with particular problems. Meditation on its own won't be a cure – you can't apply it like an ointment or take it like a medicine. But as part of an overall strategy for dealing with a particular personal problem, or to help you achieve a particular goal, it will indeed help you.

The strategy is the same in each case:
- set your goal

- make a list of all the things that are preventing you from achieving it
- meditate on these blocks to find ways of overcoming them
- use positive thinking
- act positively.

This means taking steps in your everyday routine and activities to achieve your goal, implementing the supportive groundwork done in meditation.

Be quite clear about your goal. Identify as many things as you can that are preventing you from achieving that goal. Do this before you begin any of the following meditations.

FOR BUILDING SELF-CONFIDENCE
20 minutes

— Relaxation sequence (page 25).

— Breathing technique (page 10).

— On the out-breaths, begin using the positive thinking mantra, 'I am self-confident.'

— Repeat several times.

— Imagine yourself in a situation which requires your self-confidence. Imagine your goal as clearly as you can.

— Pause.

— Meditate now on all those things — particularly feelings and thoughts — which are preventing you from achieving your goal. Explore them one by one, and in each case allow a solution to arise in your mind in their place.

— Pause.

— Say to yourself, 'I have now overcome the obstacles. I will no longer prevent myself from achieving self-confidence.'

— Repeat this.

— Imagine your goal again, and see yourself achieving it with ease.

— Pause.

— Breathing technique. Again on the out-breaths repeat the mantra, 'I am self-confident.'

— End the meditation when you are ready.

FOR STOPPING SMOKING
20 minutes

— Relaxation sequence (page 25).

— Breathing technique (page 10).

On the out-breaths begin using the positive thinking mantra, 'I no longer need to smoke.'

— Repeat several times.

— Imagine yourself in a situation in which you would normally be smoking a cigarette, but this time put yourself in that situation without one. Breathe freely.

— Pause.

— Meditate now on all those things — particularly feelings and thoughts — which are preventing you from achieving your goal. Explore them one by one, and in each case allow a solution to arise in your mind in their place.

— Pause.

— Say to yourself, 'I have now overcome the obstacles. I will no longer prevent myself from stopping smoking.'

— Repeat this.

— Imagine your goal again and see yourself achieving it with ease.

— Pause.

— Breathing technique. Again on the out-breaths repeat the mantra, 'I no longer need to smoke.'

— End the meditation when you are ready.

FOR ACHIEVING YOUR DESIRED WEIGHT
20 minutes

— Relaxation sequence (page 25).

— Breathing technique (page 10).

— On the out-breaths, begin using the positive thinking mantra, 'I have the perfect body,' or, if more appropriate, 'I love my body.'

— Repeat several times.

— Picture yourself with the physical attributes and body weight that you would like to achieve. Be quite clear about your goal.

– Pause.

– Meditate now on all those things – particularly feelings and thoughts – which are preventing you from achieving your goal. Explore them one by one and in each case allow a solution to arise in your mind in their place.

– Pause.

– Say to yourself, 'I have now overcome the obstacles. I will no longer prevent myself from achieving my desired weight.'

– Repeat this.

– Imagine your goal again and see yourself achieving it with ease.

– Pause.

– Breathing technique. Again on the out-breaths repeat the mantra, 'I have the perfect body,' or 'I love my body.'

– End the meditation when you are ready.

FOR PASSING EXAMS
20 minutes

– Relaxation sequence (page 25).

– Breathing technique (page 10).

– On the out-breaths, begin using the positive mantra, 'I will pass my exam.'

– Repeat this several times.

– Picture yourself passing the exam. Be quite clear about your goal.

– Pause.

– Meditate now on all those things – particularly feelings and thoughts – which are preventing you from achieving your goal. Explore them one by one and in each case allow a solution to arise in your mind in their place.

– Pause.

– Say to yourself, 'I have now overcome the obstacles. I will no longer prevent myself from passing my exam.'

– Repeat this.

– Imagine your goal again and see yourself achieving it with ease.

– Pause.

– Breathing technique. Again on the out-breaths repeat the mantra, 'I will pass my exam.'

– End the meditation when you are ready.

FOR IMPROVING YOUR SELF-IMAGE
20 minutes

– Relaxation sequence (page 25).

– Breathing technique (page 10).

– On the out-breaths, begin using the positive mantra, 'I am creating a positive self-image,' or 'I love myself,' if this is more appropriate.

– Repeat several times.

– Picture yourself with a strong self-image, full of self-esteem. Be quite clear about your goal.

– Pause.

– Meditate now on all those things – particularly feelings and thoughts – which are preventing you from achieving your goal. Explore them one by one and in each case allow a solution to arise in your mind in their place.

– Pause.

– Say to yourself, 'I have now overcome the obstacles. I will no longer prevent myself from having self-esteem and a positive self-image.'

– Repeat this.

– Imagine your goal again and see yourself achieving it with ease.

– Pause.

– Breathing technique. Again on the out-breaths repeat the mantra, 'I am creating a positive self-image', or, 'I love myself.'

– End the meditation when you are ready.

FOR IMPROVING RELATIONSHIPS
20 minutes

– Relaxation sequence (page 25).

– Breathing technique (page 10).

– On the out-breaths, begin using the positive mantra, 'My relationship is healed.'

– Repeat several times.

– Picture yourself with the relationship that you want. Be quite clear about your goal.

– Pause.

– Meditate now on all those things – particularly feelings and thoughts – which are preventing you from achieving your goal. Explore them one by one and in each case allow a solution to arise in your mind in their place.

– Pause.

– Say to yourself, 'I have now overcome the obstacles. I will no longer prevent myself from having the relationship that I need.'

– Repeat this.

– Imagine your goal again and see yourself achieving it with ease.

– Pause.

– Breathing technique. Again on the out–breaths repeat the mantra, 'My relationship is healed.'

– End the meditation when you are ready.

———————

FOR IMPROVING YOUR FINANCIAL CIRCUMSTANCES
20 minutes

– Relaxation sequence (page 25).

HEALING MEDITATIONS

— Breathing technique (page 10).

— On the out–breaths, begin using the positive mantra, 'I have everything I need.'

— Repeat several times.

— Picture yourself in the financial circumstances that you need to achieve.

— Be quite clear about your goal.

— Pause.

— Meditate now on all those things — particularly feelings and thoughts — which are preventing you from achieving your goal. Explore them one by one and in each case allow a solution to arise in your mind in their place.

— Pause.

— Say to yourself, 'I have now overcome the obstacles. I will no longer prevent myself from having the finances that I need.'

— Repeat this.

— Imagine your goal again and see yourself achieving it with ease.

— Pause.

— Breathing technique. Again on the out-breaths repeat the mantra, 'I have everything I need.'

— End the meditation when you are ready.

FOR ACHIEVING CAREER GOALS
20 minutes

— Relaxation sequence (page 25).

— Breathing technique (page 10).

— On the out-breaths, begin using the positive mantra, 'I am successful.'

— Repeat several times.

— Picture yourself already in a position of success in your career. Be quite clear about your goal.

— Pause.

— Meditate now on all those things — particularly feelings and thoughts — which are preventing you from achieving your goal. Explore them one by one and in each case allow a solution to arise in your mind in their place.

— Pause.

— Say to yourself, 'I have now overcome the obstacles. I will no longer prevent myself from achieving my career goals.'

— Repeat this.

— Imagine your goal again and see yourself achieving it with ease.

— Pause.

— Breathing technique. Again on the out–breaths repeat the mantra, 'I am successful.'

— End the meditation when you are ready.

The final meditation in this sequence is aimed at improving performance in whatever area might be relevant to you. In particular, I have in mind performance standards in a sport or in playing a musical instrument, where achieving high standards depends as much on your psychological preparation as it does on your level of fitness or technical ability.

FOR IMPROVING PERFORMANCE
20 minutes

— Relaxation sequence (page 25).

— Breathing technique (page 10).

— On the out–breaths, begin using the positive mantra, 'I will achieve my goal.'

— Repeat several times.

— Picture yourself having achieved the performance standard that you have set for yourself. Be quite clear about your goal.

— Pause.

— Meditate now on all those things — particularly feelings and thoughts — which are preventing you from achieving your goal.

— Explore them one by one, and in each case allow a solution to arise in your mind in their place.

— Pause.

— Say to yourself, 'I have now overcome the obstacles. I will no longer prevent myself from achieving the performance that I need.'

– Repeat this.

– Imagine your goal again and see yourself achieving it with ease.

– Pause.

– Breathing technique. Again on the out–breaths repeat the mantra, 'I will achieve my goal.'

– End the meditation when you are ready.

That is the conclusion of this sequence of meditations, but before we move on, note that you can apply the principle and pattern of these meditations to any circumstances in your life which you wish to heal or improve. During the meditation the aim is to imagine yourself having already achieved your goal, so that you can experience what it actually feels like to do this. Also, I place a lot of emphasis on being quite clear what exactly it is that you wish to achieve – and this means becoming aware of all the possible consequences, for other people as well as for yourself. If, during this process, you realise that you want to move your goals, this is all right. Don't be afraid to do so.

Now I want to turn to the healing process itself, keeping in mind the relationship that I have discussed between the polarities of mind and body, between your conscious self-awareness and the unconscious.

Colour and Crystal Healing

You are now in a position to use the ideas on colour introduced in Chapter 3, combined with the aim of bringing healing to mind and body. Try this:

CRYSTAL HEALING
25 minutes

— Relaxation sequence (page 25).

— Breathing technique (page 10).

— See in your mind's eye a clear crystal. Make it real. You can touch it and hold it. Feel the weight. Feel its surfaces against your skin. Examine it carefully.

— Pause.

— Place it in front of you so that you can see it clearly, and look into it.

— Pause.

— As you look into the crystal, it begins to glow inside with white light.

— Pause.

— The light grows until the crystal is radiating light.

— Pause.

— The light begins to change colour. First it becomes red. Let the crystal glow and emit red light.

— Pause.

— The light changes to orange.

— Pause.

— Then yellow.

– Pause.

– Now green.

– Pause.

– Changing to blue.

– Pause.

– Then indigo.

– Pause.

– Now violet.

– Pause.

– You are going to choose one of these colours and use it for healing. Choose a colour to which you are intuitively drawn, remembering that the red end of the spectrum increases energy, while the blue end is calming. Choose your colour and let the crystal respond to your choice.

– Pause.

– Let the crystal glow with your colour. . . . It is all right if you want to change it to another colour.

– Pause.

– When you feel good about the colour you have chosen, let the energy inside the crystal increase so that the intensity of the coloured light increases.

– Pause.

– Choose a part of your body which will benefit from healing energy. You can choose your whole being if you like.

– Pause.

– Let the coloured light flow into this part of your body, filling it with healing energy. You can let the healing light fill your whole being.

– Pause.

– When you are ready, let the light energy fade until you become aware again of the crystal, which is still gently glowing with your chosen colour.

– Pause.

– The colour begins to change again, first becoming red. Let the crystal glow and emit red light.

– Pause.

– The light changes to orange.

– Pause.

– Then yellow.

– Pause.

– Now green.

– Pause.

– Changing to blue.

– Pause.

— Then indigo.

— Pause.

— Now violet.

— Pause.

— Now all the colours merge until the crystal is glowing with a white light.

— Pause.

— Let the intensity of the white light increase until it radiates out, filling you, then flowing on out into the world. You are now radiating light, healing energy, into the universe so that its healing vibrations can touch everyone and everything that shares this world with you.

— Pause.

— Let the light energy subside until you see the crystal once more. Now it has stopped creating light and is still.

— Pause.

— Let the image of the crystal fade, and in its place you see a cross within a circle. This is a universal symbol of wholeness and healing. Contemplate this image and let any thoughts or feelings that arise in response flow into you.

— Pause.

— Let the image of the cross in a circle fade. Become aware of your breathing. Breathe a little more deeply than you would normally. While staying completely relaxed, become aware of your body and your environment . . . and open your eyes.

— Pause.

— Before you return to your everyday activities, spend a few more moments experiencing the after-effects of the meditation and contemplating the experience that you have just had.

— Pause.

— You can use the crystal for self-healing at any time you wish.

The symbol of a cross within a circle that you visualised at the end of this meditation is an image of wholeness and healing. The circle represents spirit surrounding the cross, which represents the material world and its dimensions.

Symbols such as the circle and the cross can be visualised to stimulate the process of healing, making whole. So can specific colours. I touched on this in Chapter 3 when I introduced the colours associated with each centre of awareness. The meditations were created to stimulate each centre through its colour correspondence. In the Crystal Healing meditation given above, I suggested that you chose a particular colour to which you felt intuitively drawn. The idea was that, after experiencing the meditation, you might want to investigate the chakra with which it is associated.

Another way to develop colour healing is to choose a particular colour, or combination of colours, based on their known qualities. Here are some of the healing properties of the main colours. The qualities of each one can be stimulated in meditation. Another approach used by colour healers, and which can be used in conjunction with meditation, is the use of coloured lighting.

RED is a stimulating colour, it can be used when your energy is low, although it should be avoided if you have a tendency towards aggression or irritation. Red is warming and can be used to increase your circulation and raise your body temperature. It stimulates desire and sexual activity. Red has an immediate effect and can increase your willpower.

ORANGE can increase your health and vitality and is generally stimulating. It can be used to alleviate depression, heaviness and lack of enthusiasm. Orange helps the process of release, bringing freedom for the expression of suppressed thoughts and feelings. It stimulates creativity and self-confidence.

YELLOW stimulates mental activity, coordination and communication. It encourages clarity of thought and freedom from obsessions. A colour associated with waking consciousness, it can be used if you don't feel fully awake, even if your sleep patterns are satisfactory.

GREEN is the colour of new life and is appropriate for use at the beginning or creation of any new project, relationship or awareness of any kind. Green stimulates emergence and growth. Its appearance in meditation can come at the point where one stage or phase of life is ending and another beginning. It represents the point of balance between polar opposites. Green awakens compassion and feelings towards others, and is appropriate for use when these qualities are lacking.

BLUE is the first of the calming colours and can be used to bring peace and tranquillity. It will stimulate your ability to let go, perhaps of outworn and inappropriate patterns of behaviour. Blue should be used when the rational mind is too strong and intuition too weak, for it will nurture the latter.

INDIGO, also at the calming end of the colour spectrum, is the colour most likely to lead to the awakening of new dimensions to life and awareness. It will stimulate your ability to visualise and channel the images, thoughts, feelings and sensations that arise from your unconscious; it will therefore also stimulate dreams and psychic activity. It is not an appropriate colour for people with over-active imaginations. The appearance of indigo in meditation suggests that expanded consciousness is not far away.

VIOLET is the colour of healing for polar opposites, bringing conscious and unconscious, inner and outer worlds of experience, mind and matter into relationship with one another. Its appearance suggests mystical or religious experience and awakening. It can be used when you want to develop humility, and also to transcend a situation. Violet has great healing qualities and brings an appreciation of the true value of things in a non-material sense. Over-concern for materialism can be compensated through healing with the colour violet.

In the Crystal Healing meditation, I did not specify a particular type of crystal to visualise. Under certain circumstances it is important to let your unconscious or intuition decide for you the shape, form and colour of the image that is presented to your mind's eye. Once you have experienced this, the following associations with different crystals and gemstones will give you more insight into the images you receive in your meditation; alternatively, use them to select a particular crystal to work with. As with colour, a crystal can be a visualised image, or you can obtain one as an outer object or talisman to stimulate a particular energy within you.

The numbers given after each gemstone indicate its associated chakra (see illustration on page 68).

AGATE (6)
Blue lace agate aids the flow of self-expression; relieves neck, shoulder and head pain; heals sore throats and neutralises inflammation. *Moss agate* improves your circulation and creates harmony.

AMBER (all chakras)
Strengthens the tissues of the central nervous system and stimulates all your glands.

AMETHYST (6, 7)
Calming and protective; it assists the process of release.

AQUAMARINE (3, 5)
Assists in achieving clarity of thought; encourages creative expression; activates the thymus; and dissipates fears and phobias.

AVENTURINE (4)
Relieves emotional stress and anxiety.

AZURITE (5, 6)
Improves visualisation; stimulates the spleen and thyroid; clears old thought patterns.

BLOODSTONE (1)
Cleansing and grounding, this stone strengthens your heart and your courage.

CALCITE (7)
Improves your memory and eyesight, assisting clear observation.

CARNELIAN (2)
Stimulates the will and relieves asthmatic symptoms.

CELESTITE (5)
Relieves tension headaches and improves communication.

CHRYSOCOLLA (4, 5)
Releases stress; reduces anger, fear and guilt; strengthens breathing and stimulates the thyroid.

CITRINE (3, 7)
Encourages the body's natural healing powers; detoxifies the system and aids regeneration; increases intuition and decreases self-destructive tendencies; lends support in breaking addictive behaviour.

DIAMOND (all chakras)
Dispels negativity and brings balance to a troubled mind; diamond has all-purpose healing properties.

EMERALD (4)
Calming for mind and emotions; strengthens the immune system.

FLUORITE (6, 7)
Aids meditation; healing for strokes and arthritis; calming and focusing; puts one in touch with the body, creating physical awareness – grounding.

GARNET (1)
Stimulates the pituitary gland and the circulation of the blood; healing for anaemia; calms thoughts and feelings – grounding.

HAWK'S EYE (1)
Encourages peace and tranquillity; said to assist the development of extra-sensory perception.

HAEMATITE (1)
Increases your resistance to stress; stimulates the spleen; encourages the process of change.

JADITE (4)
Strengthens the heart and kidneys; boosts the immune system; healing for the emotions; dispels negative patterns.

KAYANITE (5, 6)
Stimulates dreams and visualisation.

KUNZITE (4)
Assists in coping with depression; healing for broken relationships; strengthening for the heart.

LAPIS LAZULI (5, 6)
Harmonises your inner and outer life; encourages spiritual awakening; stimulates the thyroid; aids fertility; improves vitality.

MALACHITE (5, 6)
Relieves broken sleep patterns; clears unconscious energy blocks.

MOLDAVITE (6)
Stimulates the imagination and intuition.

MOONSTONE (4)
Brings emotional stability; relieves anxiety; helpful for pre-menstrual tension.

OBSIDIAN (1, 3, 7)
Stimulates vitality and the will.

PERIDOT (2, 3, 4)
Brings mental stability; accelerates personal growth; sta-bilises the emotions.

PYRITES (1, 3)
Improves digestion and elimination; strengthens the will.

QUARTZ
There are many types of quartz. For example: *rose quartz (4)* is emotionally calming; healing for the kidneys; healing for childhood traumas; and aids in forgiveness and compassion. *Smoky quartz (1)* stimulates the adrenal glands and aids depression.

RHODOCHROSITE (1, 2, 3)
Heals emotional wounds; brings self-acceptance; enhances the memory.

RUBY (1, 4)
Stimulating both to energy and the will or courage; aids emotional and physical stability; strengthens the immune system; develops spiritual devotion.

SAPPHIRE (1, 6)
Enhances intuition; calms the mind; aids the digestive process.

SELENITE (7)
Soothes the nervous system and strengthens willpower.

SODALITE (5, 6)
Reduces fear and guilt; aids self-expression; grounding.

SULPHUR (3)
Encourages clarity; strengthens the will.

TIGER'S EYE (3)
Helps deal with stubborn traits; creates flow in communication; brings insight.

TOPAZ (3, 7)
Helpful in arthritis and rheumatism; relieves anger, depression and fear; assists the digestive process.

TOURMALINE – BLACK (1)
Psychic protection from negative energies; puts one in touch with the body – grounding.

TOURMALINE – BLUE (5)
Calms anger and frustration; relieves sadness; brings inner peace; healing for sore throats.

TOURMALINE – PINK/RED (4)

Stimulates passion; encourages the inner child and the expression of youthful desires.

TOURMALINE – GREEN (4)

Anti-depressant; enhances sensitivity; beneficial for the endocrine (hormone) system.

TURQUOISE (4, 5)

Opens all centres of awareness; calming for the emotions.

The qualities associated with the crystals are guidelines with which you might like to experiment. Either visualise the crystal in or near its associated chakra, or place a real crystal on or close to the chakra while you are meditating. Finally, try this:

FULL CRYSTAL ATTUNEMENT
20 minutes

Choose seven crystals with the appropriate colour or healing properties that you would like to experience. Visualise each crystal on or near your chakras. Direct your attention to each one in turn and open yourself to experiencing their effect on you. If you have a crystal collection you could lie down and place each chosen crystal on or near the appropriate chakra before meditating on their effects. Do this for about twenty minutes. Take a careful note of your responses and adjust your choice of crystals and colours accordingly.

When dealing with the healing process the emphasis in all my meditation work is on healing as something natural, not supernatural. Meditation increases your awareness and puts you in touch with natural healing processes. Increased awareness brings to your attention those things that you are lacking or which you need in life to achieve healing. This often means becoming aware of your common sense and then acting on it. It is no good, for example, coming to an awareness of what you need and then doing nothing about it. There is a time to meditate and a time to act; both are necessary in order to achieve a balanced life.

Chapter 5 takes us on to meditations for celebrating different times of the year. This continues the theme of relating or attuning the natural inner and outer rhythms of life.

5

FESTIVAL
MEDITATIONS

Throughout the ages festivals have marked the rhythm of the yearly cycle. They have been celebrated ever since people first realised that the annual cycle of nature's growth and decay could be timed by the movement of the sun, moon and planets against the backdrop of the heavens, and in particular against the twelve signs of the zodiac.

The rituals involved do more than just mark seasonal activities. They have an effect on the human psyche, in particular on the collective human psyche, encouraging us to be aware of our relatedness and interdependence, confirming that we belong within this pattern and the unfolding story of the universe.

Such rituals have always been group activities, and the following festival meditations have a heightened effect when conducted with others. They present an opportunity for group meditation or with your family, to enhance your sense of purpose, community, and sharing in a universal experience. However, there is no reason why you should not do the meditations on your own if it suits your circumstances.

The approach to meditation so far has been one of turning away from the outside world and looking inwards, or, as I described it in Chapter 2, shifting the axis of awareness from outer world/ego self to ego self/inner world. In this chapter I want to explore the use of meditation for increasing our awareness of significant events in the outer world – the annual cycle of festivals or significant days in the cosmic calendar.

One aim of meditation is to increase awareness of our selves, which in turn heightens awareness of our relationship with the world in which we live. This means the personal relationships that we conduct with the people and events in our lives – how we 'relate' to the world in which we live. On a deeper level it means our relationship with the cycles and patterns of the natural world and with the cosmos itself.

There is a practical as well as a spiritual dimension to this. On a practical level, attunement to the annual cycle of festivals makes the individual realise his or her role as part of a whole. It is the opposite experience of alienation from society and from the world.

According to the holistic view we are part of the world, dependent on it as the source of our life, for sustaining that life, and for receiving us back when our life ends. This is the corresponding *outer* relationship to the *inner* relationship that we talked about in terms of the unconscious. The mystical view of traditional religions, which suggests the possibility of experiencing greater or different realities than our everyday world, holds that separating these inner and outer worlds is an illusion – mystical insights stress the experience of 'oneness' and this is what oneness means, namely the attunement of inner and outer universes.

Along with the decline in our religious institutions modern Western civilisation has also lost this sense of belonging in the world; it has been replaced with a growing sense of alienation. The result is loss of respect for anything that we do not regard as 'to do with me', and the decline of a healthy sense of purpose in life.

Because there is no real barrier between the inner and outer worlds, if we attune ourselves inwardly we can evoke this sense of belonging in the world. With it comes a renewed source of life's energy and purpose. Our awareness of the spiritual dimension to life grows and the role that we play in this spiritual life as individuals, each with something unique to offer, becomes more apparent.

Whether you meditate alone or in a group (see Chapter 11 for advice on how to set up and run your own meditation group), some preparation will enhance your experience of these significant cosmic events. I have adopted and adapted the suggestions given by William Bloom in his book *Sacred Times*. The process involves preparing yourself, setting up the meditation space, attuning to the space and then cleansing it, in terms of physical cleansing and inner purification. Finally, a blessing ceremony can be conducted.

As this preparation work is common to all the meditations in this chapter I will go through the sequence in detail. Feel free to leave out any parts that do not appeal to you, or to extend and adapt the preparation to suit your own purposes.

Preparation

Prepare yourself

Meditate quietly on your own for a while, perhaps contemplating the significance of the festival that you are to celebrate. A physical act of attunement such as fasting for a while can be helpful, but don't overdo it.

Prepare the meditation space

Sit for a while in the space that you will use. Become aware of its atmosphere, be open to impressions. Become aware of anything needed by this space – perhaps it needs cleaning, or brightening up with some flowers. Cleansing can be both a physical act and one of inner attunement. Simply meditate quietly in the place, focusing on the atmosphere and waiting until it feels calm and right.

You can balance and align the atmospheric energies by placing an object representing each of the four elements in each of four corners, or in the pattern of a square. The element of Earth can be represented by a bowl of salt, or a potted plant; the element of Water by a bowl of water; the element of Air by burning some incense; the element of Fire by a lighted candle. As you position each of these, practise the Capturing the Moment meditation on page 45. Position the objects, then wait until the atmosphere settles.

Taking each object in turn, contemplate the element and the essence of its meaning, and contemplate a divine being or quality which for you represents love and sharing. Imagine the blessing of this being coming into you and through you. Sense the radiation coming down through your palms and into the object that you are holding. You could then bless the object by saying something like, 'In the name of love and healing, I bless this [incense, salt, water, candle].'

Cleanse the meditation space

Prepare some water as follows. Place a bowl of water in front of you and have a few crystals of salt ready. Imagine that you place yourself at the service of what for you is a perfect being, and place your right hand out over the water. Imagine the energy of this perfect being flowing down through you and through your hand. Then take some salt crystals and release them carefully into the water. Do this three times, and as you release them you might like to say something like:

- 'I release all negative influences from this water.' Release salt.
- 'I release all negative influences from myself.' Release salt.
- 'I release all negative influences from this place.' Release salt.

Now sprinkle the water around your meditation space. This completes the preparation work.

To clear the atmosphere after a meditation you may find that making some noise works well. In a group, the chattering that naturally starts up afterwards can be sufficient, but if not, try clapping your hands or sounding a gong or chimes. You could do this right at the beginning of your preparation too, by way of an announcement of the preparation work to come, or simply to clear out the old energies and atmosphere and get things moving into the new.

Lunar Rhythms

Archaeological evidence shows that almost all prehistoric societies worshipped a Great Mother as the provider of life and the force which governed not only the visible world of nature, but also the hidden world beyond this life. No images of male gods have been discovered from the pre-Bronze Age period, but the female goddess can be found in many guises.

Mythologically, she gave a sense of the oneness of all nature, permeating everything, fructifying and nurturing, creating and destroying. She was both light and darkness, having power over life and death. Birth, life and death were regarded as a single entity, and were reflected in the continuous waxing and waning of the moon. In *The Myth of the Goddess* Anne Baring and Jules Cashford describe how 'The lunar cycle must have offered a way of comprehending how a seed grows into flower and fruit, which, falling back into the darkness of the earth, returns as the regenerated seed. . . . Spring, summer, autumn and winter parallel the waxing, full, waning and dark moon.'

So the single image which summed up nature's processes, reflecting the being of the goddess, was the moon. Today, in astrology, the moon represents the mother and the unconscious. It is a symbol of nurture and protection, ruling the emotions and feelings. One significant tie with the ancient past remains to this day: Easter Sunday, the great festival of Christian death and renewal, is fixed as the first Sunday after the first full moon following the spring equinox.

The following meditation can be conducted at the time of the full moon. This is the time in the cyclic relationship of sun and moon when they are positioned on directly opposite sides of the earth, and the full face of the moon can be seen. It is a time of heightened psychic activity and a worldwide signal for group attunement. In the annual cycle of full moons, the Taurus full moon (when the sun is in Scorpio) is also known as the Festival of Wesak, a spiritual high point of the year when, according to esoteric lore, all the illuminated beings and true spiritual teachers cooperate to invoke a great annual blessing for the earth. Some people call the following Gemini full moon (sun in Sagittarius) World Invocation Day.

FULL MOON
30 minutes

– Preparation (page 122).

– Relaxation sequence (page 25).

– Visualise the full moon.

– Pause.

– Contemplate the following and what they mean to you. Allow any thoughts, feelings or images to arise in you in reponse.
Action. Pause.
Fulfilment. Pause.
Attainment. Pause.
Completion. Pause.

– Become aware now of the flow of light, love and healing which emanates from the sun and is reflected from the moon to earth.

– Pause.

– Focus with compassion on any situation on the planet which is in need of help.

– Pause.

– Direct the flow of light, love and healing so that they radiate to where they are needed.

– Pause.

– Give thanks to the spirit of the moon.

– Pause.

– Become aware of your breathing, your body, and the room in which you are meditating. When you are ready, open your eyes.

The full moon is a time for meditating on external situations and activity, whereas the new moon is a time for inner stillness, contemplation and planning. In astrology, the full moon represents the peak of activity, attainment and completion, whereas the new moon is a symbol for releasing the old and inviting in the new. The new moon occurs when the sun and moon are aligned on the same side of the earth. None of the sun's light can be reflected off the moon's surface, which appears dark. For three nights the moon disappears from the sky.

NEW MOON
30 minutes

– Preparation (page 122).

– Relaxation sequence (page 25).

– Picture the night sky – the moon cannot be seen.

– Pause.

– Contemplate the following and what they mean to you. Allow any thoughts, feelings or images to arise in you in response.
Beginnings. Pause.
Birth. Pause.
New opportunities. Pause.
Awaiting the return. Pause.

– Meditate on those things in your life which are now outworn and no longer needed by you.

– Pause.

– Invite the new into your being and contemplate what this will mean for your future. Make your plans.

– Pause.

– Give thanks to the spirit of the moon.

– Pause.

– Become aware of your breathing, your body, and the room in which you are meditating. When you are ready, open your eyes.

The Sun and the Seasons

Let's now look at the four main celebrations of the year marked by the sun's passage through the four seasons. At the spring equinox, the sun is exactly above the Equator and the periods of day and night are equal. The sun enters the zodiacal sign of Aries and at this time, although there is a balance between day and night, the daytime forces are increasing at their quickest, heralding the sudden bursting forth of new life as spring flowers bloom.

SPRING EQUINOX
30 minutes

— Preparation (page 122).

— Relaxation sequence (page 25).

— Visualise in your mind's eye a seed. Watch the seed germinate. Watch how it puts down roots, then sends up its green shoots.

— Pause.

— Contemplate the following and what they mean to you. Allow any thoughts, feelings or images to arise in you in response.
Emergence. Pause.
Feel for the spirit of emergence. Pause.
Birth. Pause.
Feel for the spirit of birth. Pause.
Opportunity. Pause.
Feel for the spirit of opportunity. Pause.

— Become aware of these factors at work in your own life. They are at work in the outside world too and are what the forces of spring bring to the earth from the sun.

— Pause.

— Give thanks to the spirit of the sun.

– Become aware of your breathing, your body, and the room in which you are meditating, and when you are ready, open your eyes.

At the summer solstice the sun has moved to its extreme northerly point, over the Tropic of Cancer; the days are at their longest, the nights at their shortest. The sun enters the zodiacal sign of Cancer, and from now on the days will shorten and the nights lengthen. This is the time of warmth when summer is in full swing – flowers and crops are reaching their full strength and colour.

SUMMER SOLSTICE
30 minutes

– Preparation (page 122).

– Relaxation sequence (page 25).

– Picture yourself in the countryside on a warm summer's day. Take in all the many sights, sounds and smells.

– Pause.

– Contemplate the following and what they mean to you. Allow any thoughts, feelings or images to arise in you in response.
Light. Pause.
Feel for the spirit of light. Pause.
Warmth. Pause.
Feel for the spirit of warmth. Pause.
Beauty. Pause.
Feel for the spirit of beauty. Pause.
Abundance. Pause.
Feel for the spirit of abundance. Pause.

— Become aware of these factors at work in your own life. They are at work in the outside world too, and are what the forces of summer bring to the earth from the sun.

— Pause.

— Give thanks to the spirit of the sun.

— Become aware of your breathing, your body, and the room in which you are meditating. When you are ready, open your eyes.

At the autumn equinox the sun is once more directly over the Equator and the days and nights are of equal length, but the days are continually shortening and the forces of night are on the increase. The sun enters the zodiacal sign of Libra. This is the time of autumnal harvest and thanksgiving for summer crops and fruit, a time to turn our attention away from the warm, light days of summer in preparation for the winter months ahead.

AUTUMN EQUINOX
30 minutes

— Preparation (page 122).

— Relaxation sequence (page 25).

— Picture yourself working in a field, gathering in a crop — not with modern machinery, but as it used to be done long ago. There are others with you, all working hard together.

— Pause.

— Contemplate the following and what they mean to you. Allow any thoughts, feelings or images to arise in you in response.

Gathering. Pause.
Feel for the spirit of gathering. Pause.
Community. Pause.
Feel for the spirit of community. Pause.
Completion. Pause.
Feel for the spirit of completion. Pause.

– Become aware of these factors at work in your own life.
They are at work in the outside world too, and are what the
forces of autumn bring to the earth from the sun.

– Pause.

– Give thanks to the spirit of the sun.

– Become aware of your breathing, your body, and the room in
which you are meditating. When you are ready, open your eyes.

At the winter solstice the sun has moved to its extreme southerly
point, over the Tropic of Capricorn. The nights are at their longest, the days at their shortest. The sun enters the zodiacal sign of
Capricorn, and from now on the daylight hours will increase and
the nights shorten. This is the time when the forces of nature are
resting, hibernating. But even in the depths of winter new life stirs
under the ground. This is the time of nature's in-breath – the
breath is held, but on the point of release.

WINTER SOLSTICE
30 minutes

– Preparation (page 122).

– Relaxation sequence (page 25).

– Picture yourself in the middle of a wood. It is the depth of
winter. Stop and look and listen. Be aware that although

everything appears to be sleeping, it is in a state of readiness. The earth's energy is held in. There is a pause in activity, yet it is a pause full of gathering potential for the future.

— Pause.

— Contemplate the following and what they mean to you. Allow any thoughts, feelings or images to arise in you in response.
Death. Pause.
Feel for the spirit of death. Pause.
Stillness. Pause.
Feel for the spirit of stillness. Pause.
Rest. Pause.
Feel for the spirit of rest. Pause.
Protection. Pause.
Feel for the spirit of protection. Pause.

— Become aware of these factors at work in your own life. They are at work in the outside world too, and are what the forces of winter bring to the earth from the sun.

— Pause.

— Give thanks to the spirit of the sun.

— Pause.

— Become aware of your breathing, your body and the room in which you are meditating, and when you are ready open your eyes.

Fire Festivals

There are four other festivals that used to be widely cele-brated each year, and people are once again becoming aware of their significance, which can be marked with a meditative ceremony. These are the fire festivals which mark the Quarter Days of western Europe's ancient pagan Celtic tradition. These festivals acknowledge and celebrate our relationship with the earth and the spiritual unseen forces at work through the year. They are called Imbolc, on 31 January; Beltane, on 30 April; Lammas, on 31 July; and Samhain, on 31 October. The principles celebrated are of awakening (Imbolc), growth (Beltane), harvest (Lammas) and rest (Samhain).

Knowing the background to these festivals will help you in your meditations, as it explains their deeper significance. Their cycle connects us more to the moon than to the sun, and thus to the female aspect of the human soul. The fire festivals ritualised four facets of the female earth forces, each linked with a particular cycle of the moon.

The lunar year had thirteen months of about twenty-eight days per lunation cycle (from new moon to new moon). Each quarter year consists of three whole lunar months plus a quarter of a month. These festivals therefore occurred at different phases of the moon: new moon, first quarter moon, full moon and second quarter moon. In Christian times, with the domination of the calendar by the solar cycle, these festivals were fixed relative to the sun's cycle, thus disconnecting them from the moon's phases and removing their original pagan significance. They were fixed at about forty days after the solstice and equinox festivals and fall on the eves (that is, the evenings before), the 1st of the months of November, February, May and August.

Once again, for meditation purposes these festivals can be celebrated alone or in a group. They also offer an opportunity to conduct a ceremony out of doors, perhaps lighting a bonfire after your meditation to signal your awareness of your role in cooperating with the forces of nature, the earth and the cosmos. Invite your friends to be with you and share some food and drink as part of your celebration.

Imbolc is the first day of the Celtic spring and its keynote is 'awakening'. Coinciding now with Candlemass in the Christian calendar, this is a festival of kindling a new light to burn at the beginning of the new season. Candlemass is a later Christianised form of a time sacred to Brigit or Bride, the young woman facet of the goddess, who is linked with the first quarter phase of the moon. At this time there are signs of nature's stirring.

IMBOLC (Candlemass Eve, 31 January)
30 minutes

— Preparation (page 122).

— Relaxation sequence (page 25).

— Picture in your mind's eye the kindling of a flame. Then meditate on it.

— Pause.

— Contemplate the following and what it means to you. Allow any thoughts, feelings or images to arise in you in response. Awakening. Pause.

— Feel for the spirit of awakening. Pause.

— Allow the forces of awakening to come through you. Open yourself up to them and allow them in.

— Pause.

— This is the time for making resolutions and offering dedication and gifts as your contribution to the cooperating forces of nature as they come together again in the yearly round.

— What is your resolution? Pause.

— Allow it to arise in your awareness. Pause.

— What gift can you offer? Pause.

— Allow it to arise in your awareness. Pause.

— Give thanks as you once more picture the flame and its light before you.

— Pause.

— Become aware of your breathing, your body and the place in which you are meditating. When you are ready, open your eyes.

Beltane heralds the month of May, when all the hard work of preparation has been completed and the forces of growth are at work. The keynote is 'growth', and the call is for continued cooperation and protection to ensure that this growth continues successfully. It is a time for expressing gratitude that this cooperation is being given. Beltane, the eve of May Day, relates to the impregnated goddess, and therefore has much to do with fertility. The associated phase of the moon is full.

BELTANE (May Eve, 30 April)
30 minutes

— Preparation (page 122).

— Relaxation sequence (page 25).

— Picture in your mind's eye the kindling of a flame. Then meditate on it.

— Pause.

– Contemplate the following and what it means to you. Allow any thoughts, feelings or images to arise in you in response. Growth. Pause.

– Feel for the spirit of growth. Pause.

– This is a time for seeking cooperation and protection so that the forces generating fertility can continue to do their work. Open yourself to cooperation. Pause.
Ask for protection. Pause.
Meditate on the meaning and workings of fertility both in you and in nature. Pause.

– Give thanks as you once more picture the flame and its light before you.

– Pause.

– Become aware of your breathing, your body and the place in which you are meditating. When you are ready, open your eyes.

Lammas comes at the beginning of the harvest season. Its keynote is harvest and it is associated with the ripening and fruiting process. The fires of thanksgiving are lit once more to celebrate the mother goddess who gives birth to her fruit. The moon phase with which this is associated is the third quarter.

LAMMAS (August Eve, 31 July)
30 minutes

– Preparation (page 122).

– Relaxation sequence (page 25).

– Picture in your mind's eye the kindling of a flame. Then meditate on it.

– Pause.

– Contemplate the following and what it means to you. Allow any thoughts, feelings or images to arise in you in response. Harvest. Pause.

– Feel for the spirit of harvest. Pause.

– This is the time for ripening, fruiting and preparation for the harvest. Open yourself to the forces of ripening and fruiting, so that they can do their work through you and in the world.

– Pause.

– Meditate on the process of ripening.

– Pause.

– Give thanks as you once more picture the flame and its light before you.

– Pause.

– Become aware of your breathing, your body and the place in which you are meditating. When you are ready, open your eyes.

Samhain is now commonly celebrated as Hallowe'en, the night when a gateway through to the 'otherworld' opens and it is said that communication with the spirits of the dead is possible. This superstition has outlived the original significance of the Samhain fire festival, whose keynote is rest. Coming at the end of the agricultural cycle, in fact it marks the beginning of the Celtic New Year. The nature spirits now withdraw from their work and begin a period of rest and inner contemplation. This is the eve of Hecate, the old woman facet of the goddess, associated with the new moon phase.

SAMHAIN
(Hallowe'en or November Eve, 31 October)
30 minutes

— Preparation (page 122).

— Relaxation sequence (page 25).

— Picture in your mind's eye the kindling of a flame. Then meditate on it.

— Pause.

— Contemplate the following and what it means to you. Allow any thoughts, feelings or images to arise in you in response.

— Rest. Pause.

— Feel for the spirit of rest. Pause.

— This is the time for reflection on the past and preparation for the future — a gathering in of one's own forces which can then rest and regenerate; a preparation for the next cycle. Meditate on the meaning and purpose of rest.

— Pause.

— Give thanks as you once more picture the flame and its light before you.

— Pause.

— Become aware of your breathing, your body and the place in which you are meditating. When you are ready, open your eyes.

This concludes the fire festival meditations. There are many communal events for which you could prepare meditations of your own, based on the approach that I have presented here. For example, I suggested the possibility of family meditations and this could be applied to celebrations that you could devise for births, marriages and deaths. Also, whether or not you practise a particular religion you can mark through meditation the main religious festivals of the year, choosing those that are appropriate for your own beliefs and background. Even though I am not a practising Christian in the traditional sense and do not go to church services, I see good reasons for marking the festivals of Easter and Christmas, for example. Their spirit is universal, and this is why meditation at sacred times brings forth a sense of universality, belonging and participation.

At the beginning of this chapter I mentioned how festivals and natural turning-points of the year are linked with the movement of the sun and moon as they progress through the zodiac. In Chapter 6 we will look a little closer at this process through twelve meditations on the signs of the zodiac.

6

MEDITATIONS
ON THE ZODIAC

Twelve Personality Types

One of the most important reasons for meditating is to get to know yourself better – to discover your strengths and weaknesses and in particular your needs. One method that can be explored effectively involves the personality types associated with the twelve signs of the zodiac.

When astrology first developed, during the time of ancient Babylon's astronomer-priests, an attempt was made to develop an accurate calendar, timed by the seasonal movement of the sun through what we now call the signs of the zodiac. Since that time the zodiac has developed into twelve individual signs, each with a personality of its own. So the zodiac represents a perfect relationship between the inner world of human personality and the outer world of nature and its annual cycle.

A cyclic story is told by a journey through the zodiac, beginning in Aries and ending in Pisces. To continue the theme of Chapter 5, which was to create an awareness of our relationship with the cyclic patterns of nature, we are now going to take that journey around the zodiac. I will describe each of the twelve personalities so that you can use these descriptions as the basis for meditation, to learn more about these parts of your self – of your own personality.

Although we usually identify ourselves with a particular sign of the zodiac, the one in which the sun was positioned at the time of our birth, we all contain a little of every sign to a lesser or greater degree. Do not assume, therefore, that you will be able to identify yourself as one of the twelve types that I will describe. You will, however, begin to build up a picture of the prominent characteristics and begin to recognise yourself as Taurean, Sagittarian, Piscean and so on. To know yourself completely, you will need to identify traces of every sign in yourself and see how they all work.

Each sign of the zodiac has particular affinities or correspondences with parts of the body, professions, different activities and objects of all sorts, including gemstones and colours. Each sign is also associated with a particular planet. In mythology, personalities have been associated with the planets, and these will be the subject of meditations and inner journeys taken in Chapter 7.

From Astrology to Psychology

Traditional astrology is regarded by many people today as something outdated, with no relevance for the secular, materialistic society in which now live. It seems laughable to suggest that the planets and stars might emit some sort of ray that controls our everyday lives, for example, and although some astrologers still believe that our destinies are written in the stars, astrology as a subject worthy of serious study virtually disappeared with the rise of science and rationalism. But although few people take astrology seriously it is still a popular subject, for every tabloid newspaper and many magazines carry potted horoscopes.

However, serious astrology is making a comeback, though in a very different form. The increasing interest in psychology in the late twentieth century is partly responsible, and Carl Jung, the founder of analytical or 'depth' psychology, is often quoted as having had an influence on this development. Instead of astrology looking outward to the stars and planets for an understanding of how our lives are influenced by our place in the universe, it has begun to look inward, to explore the inner universe of the human psyche. This is precisely what we are doing through the meditation experience.

When you meditate on and explore the signs of the zodiac, you are exploring your inner universe. The descriptions which follow can be used as the basis for meditations in which you can picture or meditate on the particular qualities that I describe, find out how you respond to them, and look for them in your own personality. Each description will begin by placing the zodiacal sign in a context of nature's annual cycle, followed by its personality traits and key qualities.

Aries

The sun is in Aries between 20 March and 20 April. In the yearly cycle, Aries contains all the latent force of the previous year, is the seed germinating for the coming year, and gives birth to everything in nature. The *symbol* for Aries is the ram's head, and its *ruling planet* is Mars. Aries is a Fire sign, and the first sign in the circle of the zodiac. It symbolises new beginnings.

The associated *keywords* are: impulsive, pioneering, spontaneous, direct, decisive, energetic, foolhardy, courageous, opinionated, egotistical and perceptive. The *physical qualities* of Aries are: long neck, bony or angular face, broad temples, narrow chin, grey or greyish-brown eyes and wiry hair – sometimes sandy, sometimes very dark. The *mental qualities* are: ambitious, courageous, impulsive, desiring prominence, enterprising, ingenious and audacious.

The Aries *personality* is full of energy and enthusiasm, especially for new projects and ideas. Aries' responses are purely instinctive, with little thought for the consequences of what they say or do. Their trademark is achievement of their aims, but at the expense of other people. The Aries personality type is pioneering and an energetic leader. It is naive and forceful, never considering the consequences of its actions, always initiating, never finishing whatever it starts. Aries is a brash and youthful spirit. *Type*: the pioneer.

Aries rules the cerebral system, the head and all of the main organs associated with it, especially the eyes. *Gemstones* ruled by Aries are the bloodstone, coral, diamond and all minerals of a reddish hue. It is associated with the *colour* red.

Taurus

The sun is in Taurus between 20 April and 21 May. In the yearly cycle, Taurus begins to give form to the new life that emerged in Aries. Roots are established which will provide nourishment for the rest of the yearly cycle. The *symbol* for Taurus is the bull and its *ruling planet* is Venus. Taurus is an Earth sign, and the second sign in the circle of the zodiac. It symbolises foundations.

The associated *keywords* are: steadfast, loyal, dependable, determined, strong, practical, considerate, appreciative, generous, productive, stubborn, sensual and aloof. The *physical qualities* of Taurus are: strong neck and shoulders, pensive brows, full lips and nostrils, curling or wavy hair, full forehead, dark eyes and heavy jaw. The *mental qualities* are: amorous, passionate, determined, laborious, patient, proud and obstinate.

The Taurean *personality* can express great strength of purpose, loyalty and determination. In its negative form it can result in the 'bull in a china shop' mentality, but on the other hand Taurus often expresses great sensitivity to beauty, whether in nature or in the arts. The Taurus personality type is down to earth, consistent and forceful. It has a practical nature and a concern for values, whether material, artistic or spiritual. Taurus can be stubborn, as well as dependable and courageous. It has a concern for establishing firm foundations. *Type*: the pragmatist.

Taurus rules the neck, throat and ears and has an affinity with the lymphatic system of the body. The thyroid gland also comes under its influence. *Gemstones* ruled by Taurus are the sapphire, emerald and topaz. It is associated with the *colour* green.

Gemini

The sun is in Gemini between 21 May and 21 June. In the yearly cycle, Gemini is the time when summer begins. Nature is in full bloom and approaching the peak of its external activity. The *symbol* for Gemini is the twins, and its *ruling planet* is Mercury. Gemini is an Air sign, and the third sign in the circle of the zodiac. It symbolises communication.

The associated *keywords* are: intellectual, versatile, communicative, fickle, analytical, dexterous, adaptable, excitable, indiscriminate, restless. *The physical qualities* of Gemini are: tall, slender and elegant; long fingers, straight nose, wide forehead, long face, and often expressive eyes. The *mental qualities* are: learned, dexterous in the manual crafts, inventive, curious, subtle, eloquent in speech or writing, and much occupied.

The Gemini *personality* will enthusiastically explore any possibilities that are presented to it. Gemini, proficient at analysing and categorising information of all kinds, does this in an intellectual fashion. Gemini is easily distracted, like a cat that will begin a task and then suddenly change direction. The Gemini personality type is fickle, light-hearted and versatile, constantly gathering facts and telling others about them. Gemini is dexterous and can generate ideas, but will leave it to others to deal with the practicalities. *Type:* the researcher.

Gemini rules the hands, arms and lungs. *Gemstones* ruled by Gemini are beryl, agate, garnet, topaz, aquamarine, marble, chrysolite and all striped stones. It is associated with the *colour* yellow.

Cancer

The sun is in Cancer between 21 June and 23 July. In the yearly cycle, the pattern of growth is now well established and, beginning with the summer solstice, a period of consolidation begins after the rushing life-force of spring. The force of the yearly cycle is subdued and mellowed. The *symbol* for Cancer is the crab. In the early history of astrology it was represented by a tortoise (Babylon) and the scarab (Egypt). Cancer's *ruling planet* is the moon. Cancer is a Water sign, and the fourth sign in the circle of the zodiac. It symbolises nurturing. The associated *keywords* are: emotional, moody, tenacious, protective, sociable, thick-skinned, sympathetic, impressionable, psychic and clannish. The *physical qualities* of Cancer are: broad forehead, wide chest, rounded body and a laborious walk, sometimes rolling or swaying; the figure is often top-heavy; the hands and feet are small and the eyes are grey. The *mental qualities* are: changeable, roving disposition, ambitious, inclined to public life, prudent, sympathetic, imaginative and romantic.

The Cancer *personality* will always lend a sympathetic ear and be a shoulder to cry on. Never meeting situations head on, Cancer will take an indirect route. Decisions made or allegiances formed will be clung to and defended ferociously. All activities are based on feelings and emotions, hence the developed psychic faculty. Cancer is the archetypal protective mother, providing a secure home, congenial surroundings and support. It is soft and receptive but also tenacious, especially when on the defence. *Type*: the mother.

Cancer rules the breasts and chest. *Gemstones* ruled by Cancer are selenite, pearl, emerald, turquoise, onyx and all soft white stones. It is associated with the *colour* blue.

Leo

The sun is in Leo between 23 July and 23 August. In the yearly cycle, Leo represents the culmination of the creative life-force when summer is at its peak and can demonstrate the results of its creative endeavours. The *symbol* for Leo is the lion and its *ruling planet* is the sun. Leo is a Fire sign, and the fifth sign in the circle of the zodiac. It symbolises creativity.

The associated *keywords* are: leadership, loyalty, pride, strength, creativity, theatricality, demonstrativeness, overbearingness, courage, sincerity, egotism and hedonism. The *physical qualities* of Leo are: strong, broad shoulders, upright walk, cheerful expression, fearless eyes, generally of a grey tint, and wavy hair. The *mental qualities* are: faithful, proud, fearless, ambitious, generous, artistic, opposed to cliques and secrecy, oblivious to enmity, rich in life and feeling.

The Leo *personality* can be the best of friends and the worst of enemies – strong loyalties in friendship are formed, but reconciliation with enemies is not a concept that Leo entertains. Qualities of leadership, flamboyance and a love of the theatrical can make Leo a lovable character or a pain in the neck, depending on your view. The Leo personality type is the play actor and can perform a role to the hilt, provided recognition and admiration is forthcoming from an audience. Leo loves to have friends and displays loyalty and enthusiasm, demanding these in return. It has difficulty in adapting to others, and must do things its own way. *Type*: the actor or actress.

Leo rules the heart, blood and circulation. *Gemstones* ruled by Leo are: ruby, diamond, gold, chrysolite and all soft yellow minerals. It is associated with the *colour* orange.

Virgo

The sun is in Virgo between 23 August and 23 September. In the yearly cycle, Virgo represents the time before the harvest, when the fruit is ripening in the summer sunshine. Virgo represents the earth's fecundity, the fulfilment of its purpose. The *symbol* for Virgo is the virgin, traditionally depicted carrying a sheaf of corn. The ruling planet is Mercury. Virgo is an Earth sign, and the sixth sign in the circle of the zodiac. It symbolises service.

The associated *keywords* are: perfectionist, productive, organised, critical, unassuming, unselfish, self-reliant, indecisive, superficial, nervous and practical. The *physical qualities* of Virgo are: full forehead; hair generally swept back and falling about the ears, inclined to baldness, grey or blue eyes, straight nose, wide shoulders, active walk and quiet voice. The *mental qualities* are: learned, searching after knowledge, methodical, inclined to art and literature, benevolent, fond of the occult, disposed to collecting in some form or other, critical and precise.

In the Virgo *personality* two extremes can be represented – either a person meticulous in habits and appearance, or one of slovenly habit and appearance. The Virgo personality is outwardly undistinguished and unassuming, despite the important and responsible works that will be undertaken. Virgo is to be relied upon to bring forth the fruits of their labours, but will claim no credit for doing so. Virgo's methods may appear over-perfectionist, but they get results. The Virgo personality type gives service to others in any practical way possible, and will sacrifice its own needs for the needs of others. Virgo can show great discrimination and attention to detail, but can also be critical and nit-picking. It will turn its hand to most chores, no matter how mundane and unsung. *Type*: the servant.

Virgo rules the intestines, the stomach and digestive system. *Gemstones* ruled by Virgo are: jasper, topaz, aquamarine, and flint. It is associated with the *colour* yellow.

Libra

The sun is in Libra between 23 September and 23 October. In the yearly cycle, Libra represents the balancing point of the year when the days and nights are of equal length and the earth begins to prepare once more for the cold winter months ahead. The harvest is now gathered and should be shared for the benefit of all. The *symbol* for Libra is the scales, and its *ruling planet* is Venus. Libra is an Air sign, and the seventh sign in the circle of the zodiac. It symbolises balance.

The associated *keywords* are: relationship-oriented, mediating, physically loving, good at partnerships, sociable, refined, uncommitted, tactful, beautiful, gregarious, charming and indecisive. The *physical qualities* of Libra are: tall, elegant figure, putting on weight towards the prime of life; blue eyes and fair skin, which becomes ruddy or pimpled in mature years; fine brown hair, good teeth and fingernails; Grecian type. The *mental qualities* are: genial and kind-natured, with a happy disposition; fond of show and of approbation; just, persuasive, imitative, artistic, neat, orderly and amorous, but also fickle.

The dominant characteristics of the Libra *personality* are a need for harmony, especially in human relationships. Libra will go out of the way to achieve this, without becoming committed to any one point of view. Beauty and good taste in all spheres of life are high on the list of priorities. The signs from Aries to Virgo are in the 'personal' sphere of the zodiac, and their concerns are mainly with the self. Libra is the first of the six 'social' signs, and shows flair in this sphere. The Libra personality type is the diplomat, seeking justice, keen to look after the interests of all parties, and promoting the development of relationships. It is known for its ability to weigh up pros and cons before making decisions based on rational judgement. Libra is sociable and a match-maker. It shows no aggression in relationships, knowing when and when not to take the initiative. *Type*: the genial host or hostess.

Libra rules the kidneys and loins. *Gemstones* ruled by Libra are: white marble, white quartz, opal, alabaster, beryl, chrysolite and white jade. It is associated with the *colour* indigo.

Scorpio

The sun is in Scorpio between 23 October and 22 November. In the yearly cycle, Scorpio is the time when nature dies, or appears to do so. All life energy is returned to the earth in readiness for the process of regeneration. In many ways this is the end of the year, and therefore the beginning of the next. The *symbol* for Scorpio is the scorpion (also the eagle and the dove) and its ruling planet is Pluto (traditionally, Mars). Scorpio is a Water sign, and the eighth in the circle of the zodiac. It symbolises death and regeneration.

The associated *keywords* are: intense, transforming, charismatic, powerful, magnetic, manipulative, destructive, inspirational, healing and seductive. The *physical qualities* of Scorpio: dark or dusky complexion, curly dark hair, aquiline features, prominent brows and sharp facial angles. The *mental qualities* are: bold, self-confident; fond of contests and strife, very daring when put to the test; sarcastic, wilful, impulsive and determined; of fixed views and subtle mind; not easily imposed upon, but sometimes capable of imposition; frequently has a fondness for mystery.

Scorpio *personality*: the intensity of emotional expression represented by this sign results in passion which can be easily used for good or bad. Scorpio is able to influence others and will dominate through charisma. Emotional intensity may be held within, giving an air of secrecy. The Scorpio type is concerned with hidden depths, with what lies beneath surface appearances, and is intense and tenacious. There is a concern for the hidden, the secretive. Scorpio will always find more to a situation than meets the eye, being able to bring regeneration to all that it touches. *Type*: the power-seeker.

Scorpio rules the sexual organs. *Gemstones* ruled by Scorpio are: ruby, topaz, malachite, jasper and vermilion. It is associated with the *colour* red.

Sagittarius

The sun is in Sagittarius between 22 November and 22 December. In the yearly cycle Sagittarius is the time of short days and long nights, when the winter solstice is approaching – a time for contemplation rather than action. Nature is stilled and all activity ceases in preparation for the depths of winter. The *symbol* for Sagittarius is the centaur, half man, half beast, depicted as an archer. Its ruling planet is Jupiter. Sagittarius is a Fire sign, and the ninth sign in the circle of the zodiac. It symbolises the search for meaning in life.

The associated *keywords* are: philosophical, expansive, jovial, open-minded, explorative, adventurous, sporting, freedom-loving, prone to exaggeration, impractical, judgemental and straightforward. The *physical qualities* of Sagittarius are: tall, well-made figure, but sometimes stooping; rather long face; fine, rounded forehead; usually grey or blue eyes, sometimes brown, but always expressive; good complexion; frequently bald about the temples; fond of athletic exercise. The *mental qualities* are: generous, good-tempered, just, frank and a firm friend; inclined to philosophy and religion; eclectic; not much inclined to exact sciences; fond of travelling.

The Sagittarius *personality* is at home with philosophy and abstract thought, needing to solve ever-deeper mysteries in life. The understanding that this brings creates an inspirational teacher who backs up theories with the fruits of experience. Sagittarius will seek this in any way possible, from material to spiritual pursuits, often over-indulging in them. Sagittarius is the epitome of honesty, wishing only to enlighten others with insights into the nature of reality. The Sagittarius personality type is optimistic, open to experience and adventure. Never satisfied with current achievements, it constantly aims for distant goals and strives for the unattainable. It likes to deal with big ideas and projects, often those with no practical foundation. *Type*: the guide.

Sagittarius rules the liver, hips and thighs. *Gemstones* ruled by Sagittarius are: turquoise, amethyst, topaz, carbuncle and all stones mixed with red and green. It is associated with the *colour* light blue.

Capricorn

The sun is in Capricorn between 22 December and 20 January. In the yearly cycle Capricorn is the gateway to the new year, beginning at the winter solstice. The *symbol* for Capricorn is the goat, sometimes depicted as the goat fish or sea goat. Capricorn's *ruling planet* is Saturn. It is an Earth sign, and the tenth sign in the circle of the zodiac. Capricorn symbolises the building of structures.

The associated *keywords* are: methodical, persistent, self-effacing, traditional, dour, industrious, organising, ambitious, opportunistic, dictatorial, trustworthy, loyal, prudent, persevering and responsible. The *physical qualities* of Capricorn are: prominent features; long nose, frequently bent inward at the point; firm lips, strong but narrow chin; thin neck; and dark, thin hair. The *mental qualities* are:

wilful, strong in purpose, very ambitious, keen to have the upper hand, capricious; reserved; quiet and reclusive, but forceful in action.

The significant point about the Capricorn *personality* is that personal concerns never come first, whether in a political context (the state matters more than the individual) or in a business one, when everything is done for the benefit of the company, not the individuals in it. Even in personal relationships, Capricorn's approach is essentially pragmatic and leaves nothing to chance. Ambitions are usually achieved through persistence and hard work, rather than inspiration. The Capricorn personality type is the empire-builder, erector of systems and structures, ambitious, paternal and authoritative. Capricorn will bring the ideas of others to fruition – will make them work. Success comes to Capricorn in the fullness of time, not overnight. It has a concern for the maintenance of traditional values and will stamp its authority on all its deeds. Capricorn is a captain of industry. *Type*: the figure of authority.

Capricorn rules the skin, the skeleton and the teeth. *Gemstones* ruled by Capricorn are: onyx, jet, sapphire, coal, and all black or ash-coloured minerals. It is associated with the *colour* green.

Aquarius

The sun is in Aquarius between 20 January and 18 February. In the yearly cycle, the first sense of the end of the astrological cycle appears. There is one more sign, Pisces, but first the depths of winter must be survived. The *symbol* for Aquarius is the water-bearer. Aquarius is known as the sign of humanity. Its ruling *planet* is Uranus (traditionally Saturn). Aquarius is an Air sign, and the eleventh sign in the circle of the zodiac. It symbolises brotherhood and sisterhood.

The associated *keywords* are: humanitarian, idealistic,

revolutionary, inventive, sociable, gregarious, concerned, influential, reforming, fanatical, cold, aloof and intuitive. The *physical qualities* are: tall, full figure; fine, clear complexion, blue eyes, oval face. This sign, next to Libra, is associated with physical beauty. The *mental qualities* are: kind, humane, fond of music and science, loves humanising influences and makes many friends.

The Aquarius *personality* is the revolutionary of the zodiac, whose humanitarian ends justify the means. Operating naturally in a group, Aquarius will make as many enemies as friends through his or her outspoken ideals. Despite having many friends, Aquarius is not at home in a one-to-one relationship, and can appear cold and unemotional. The Aquarius personality type has a greater affinity with people in general than with individuals. All their actions are done in the name of humanity. Aquarius is the innovator, the eccentric, the visionary and social reformer, with a cause to promote; it will follow a cause, a political ideal, to the end. *Type*: the visionary.

Aquarius rules the ankles, the calves and the blood circulation. *Gemstones* ruled by Aquarius are: blue sapphire, black pearl, obsidian and slate. It is associated with the *colour* orange.

Pisces

The Sun is in Pisces between 18 February and 20 March. In the yearly cycle we have come to the final stage in the astrological story. The *symbol* for Pisces is the two fishes, and its *ruling planet* is Neptune (traditionally Jupiter). Pisces is a Water sign, and the twelfth and last sign in the circle of the zodiac. It symbolises sacrifice.

The associated *keywords* are: self-reflective, emotionally sensitive, psychic, imaginative, innovative, strongly aspirational, paranoid, self-deluding, experimental, unselfish and self-denying. The *physical qualities* are: short stature; fully-fleshed body; small hands and feet, short limbs; dark complexion. The *mental qualities* are: loquacious, cheerful, changeable, passionate; secretive in many things; difficult to know; generally disposed to a double life; quick in understanding; versatile.

The Pisces *personality* is the artistic temperament. Living on emotional energy, Pisces can have a poor sense of self-identity, resulting in acts of self-sacrifice for the good of the whole, or, on the negative side, the waste of abilities and talents which always come to nothing. Pisces is the mystic and the visionary, whose concern is never for this world but for the one beyond its material boundaries. The Pisces personality type is a peace-loving dreamer, with an over-active and impressionable imagination. Pisces is the inspired artist, imaginative but often lacking in practical application. Imaginative to the point of being psychically sensitive, Pisceans often have difficulty discerning the real from the imaginary. *Type*: the dreamer.

Pisces rules the feet and the pituitary gland, sometimes referred to as 'the third eye'. *Gemstones* ruled by Pisces are: chrysolite, coral, pumice, topaz and amethyst. It is associated with the *colour* magenta.

7

INNER JOURNEYS

In this chapter you will have the opportunity to make full use of your imagination in your meditations. We are going to explore images taken from mythology and astrology and combine them with the meditation techniques that you have learnt so far. However, if what you want from meditation is simply a means of relaxation and stress relief, this part of the book might not be for you because it explores a little further than the surface of the inner world.

As we have seen, in the healing process visualised images and symbols form a bridge between the conscious self and the unconscious. Now the bridge can be built using the knowledge and experience that have been presented in previous chapters.

The planets of our solar system have the names of Roman gods and goddesses, while the sun and moon are also associated mythologically with particular deities. To the ancients Venus and Mars, for example, were real, living beings with individual personalities and characteristics. They had particular powers or attributes and would behave in certain ways.

Jungian psychology describes how these gods are no longer regarded as living outside us but are what it describes as archetypes (see page 228). Venus, for instance, the mythological goddess of love, would behave in a certain way, and you can learn about her behaviour patterns by reading the myths about her. Venus as an archetype reveals how we as human beings conduct the story of our own loves and relationships – what drives us, not from without, but from within, from the unconscious.

Astrology tells us even more about what the planetary gods or archetypes represent. For example, the moon represents our emotional, feeling natures. In this sense, the planets each reflect a specific part of our personalities.

In each of the following meditations I have chosen a mythological character associated with a planet and described the part of the personality which this particular symbol represents, together with some of its mythological associations. You then choose which aspect of yourself you would like to explore, and go through the meditation.

You will visualise the particular planet as a person – in just the same way as, say, the ancient Greeks would have pictured Venus, Mars or Jupiter. Each meditation is introduced with information about the particular mythological image which it employs. You can find out more by reading the myths themselves.

Each meditation can become a journey. They all begin with The Garden, described in Chapter 1. I have included only outline suggestions after that point, but you might like to take them further by spending more time on them and allowing the images to develop in whatever direction they will.

You could use the format of the meditations in conjunction with any mythological character. I have chosen the basic ones of moon, Mercury, Venus, Mars, Jupiter, Saturn and the sun. Until relatively recent times these were the only seven planets known to humans.

If you have tried some of the earlier meditations you may be feeling a little mystified about what should be happening to you and what you should be experiencing. Whatever your experience is, that's fine. However, it sometimes helps to know what other people experience when meditating on the same themes. An advantage of meditating in a group is that the results can be shared and discussed afterwards. So, to give you this kind of insight, each of the following meditations ends with a brief repeat from the point of view of the meditator. To arrive at this situation, while writing I went through each of the meditations myself and wrote down a summary of my experiences.

Your own experiences won't be the same at all, but you will get an idea of the possibilities and you will see the sort of information that can be recorded when keeping a diary of your inner journeys (see page 229). The notes I have made are very brief; yours could be much fuller, especially if you write down thoughts and realisations that occur to you as you are doing so.

These meditations can be quite revealing and, as with all meditations, should be an enjoyable experience. But always follow the golden rule – if it feels right, fine. If not, then don't do it.

THE MOON
20 minutes

The moon is a symbol representing emotions, feelings, the mother and the unconscious. It contributes to emotional sensitivity and the way we respond to experiences, both outer and inner. The moon has a lot to do with your personality and the way that you adapt to changing circumstances. It represents the feminine principle and has attributes of nurturing and protection. It also rules the natural forces of growth, decay and rebirth. Strong likes, dislikes and prejudices are attributed to the moon. Its constructive qualities are sensitivity, sympathy, protection and affection. Its negative qualities are moodiness, unreliability, being wilfully destructive and easily influenced. In prehistoric culture the moon was a great symbol for life and death. Everything was born out of her and everything returned to her at the end of life in a never-ending cycle, represented by the phases of the moon.

In Greek mythology, several goddesses such as Artemis,

Astarte, Demeter, Hera and Hecate were associated with the moon. Hera, the wife of Zeus, represents that aspect of the feminine which is attracted to male power. These goddesses all had Roman counterparts. For example, to the Romans Artemis was Diana, the virgin huntress.

— Relaxation sequence (page 25).

— Imagine that you are in a garden (see the Inner Garden on page 46). This is not a garden that you know in your outer life, but one that you create in your imagination. Really be there, looking at any flowers, shrubs or trees that may be growing. The garden is enclosed by a high wall. Spend a little time getting to know the garden.

— Pause.

— In the garden there is a particular place with a special atmosphere, a focal point to which you are drawn. Go to this place. Look around you and sense the atmosphere.

— Pause.

— This is a protected place, where no one and nothing may enter without your permission.

— Pause.

— Imagine that you invite the moon into your garden. Imagine that the moon comes to you as a person.

— Pause.

— Build up a picture in your mind of the moon as a person. What is the moon wearing? What does the moon look like?

— Pause.

— How is the moon responding to you, and how do you feel about or react to the moon?

— Pause.

— Spend a little time building up an image of the moon. Take whatever comes to you, and allow the image to change and grow if it wishes to do so.

— Pause.

— Imagine that you greet the moon and begin to talk together. What does the moon want to say to you?

— Pause.

— Spend time getting to know the moon's personality. What qualities and special powers does the moon have?

— Pause.

— Ask the moon to give you a gift or symbol, something that represents your need from the moon. Take whatever occurs to you first, and ask the moon to explain the meaning of the gift.

— Pause.

— What should you do with the gift and how should you use it?

— Pause.

— Is there anything else that the moon would like to say to you or show you — particularly about your emotional, feeling nature?

— Pause.

— When you are ready, thank the moon for being with you and then let the image fade until you are alone again in the garden.

— Pause.

— Contemplate all that has just happened to you.

— Pause.

— When you are ready, let the image of the garden fade and become aware of your breathing. Become aware of your body and the place in which you are meditating, and open your eyes.

Meditation diary

This is an extract from my experience of the above meditation.

The garden was well kept and formal in design, with high hedges, grassy walkways and imposing old yew trees. It was dusk, almost dark in fact, so that everything was shadowy and mysterious. When I invited the moon to appear, it was a woman whose image formed quite quickly and, in contrast with the dusk, she was wearing white robes which actually radiated light.

When I came close to the moon and greeted her, I came within the aura of this light and somehow I started to radiate it too. The moon was very welcoming and affectionate towards me. She gave me a gift of a tall, thin, pyramid-shaped crystal which began to melt like ice when I held it. I took this to mean that I was emotionally cold and needed to melt or warm up a little. When I asked the moon about this she agreed and said that there were a lot of feelings that I needed to express. The melting pyramid was a symbol of this need. When the image of the moon faded at the end, I was left still with the glowing light inside myself, which made me feel good.

MERCURY
20 minutes

Mercury (Hermes in Greek mythology) is the winged messenger of the gods. He represents our ability to communicate
and to coordinate – in other words, the rational mind and the
way we think. The constructive qualities of Mercury are skill,
versatility and shrewdness, whereas his negative traits are
cunning, meddlesomeness, inconsistency and deceptiveness.
Mercury also has an association with thieves and pranksters.
Jung called the archetype, which he said had much in common
with Mercury, the Trickster. In mythology, Mercury was
exceptionally cunning but was also known as the healer god,
as well as being the messenger between the gods, mortals
and the underworld of the dead.

– Relaxation sequence (page 25).

– Imagine that you are in a garden (see the Inner Garden on
page 46). This is not a garden that you know in your outer life,
but one that you create in your imagination. Really be there,
looking at any flowers, shrubs or trees that may be growing.
The garden is enclosed by a high wall. Spend a little time
getting to know the garden.

– Pause.

– In the garden there is a particular place with a special
atmosphere, a focal point to which you are drawn. Go to this
place. Look around you and sense the atmosphere.

– Pause.

– This is a protected place, where no one and nothing may
enter without your permission.

– Pause.

– Imagine that you invite Mercury into your garden. Imagine that Mercury comes to you as a person.

– Pause.

– Build up a picture in your mind of Mercury as a person. What is Mercury wearing? What does Mercury look like?

– Pause.

– How is Mercury responding to you, and how do you feel about or react to Mercury?

– Pause.

– Spend a little time building up an image of Mercury. Take whatever comes to you, and allow the image to change and grow if it wishes to do so.

– Pause.

– Imagine that you greet Mercury and begin to talk together. What does Mercury want to say to you?

– Pause.

– Spend time getting to know Mercury's personality. What qualities and special powers does Mercury have?

– Pause.

– Ask Mercury to give you a gift or symbol, something that represents your need from Mercury. Take whatever occurs to you first, and ask Mercury to explain the meaning of the gift.

– Pause.

— What should you do with the gift and how should you use it?

— Pause.

— Is there anything else that Mercury would like to say to you or show you — particularly about the way that you communicate with other people?

— Pause.

— When you are ready, thank Mercury for being with you and then let the image fade until you are alone again in the garden.

— Pause.

— Contemplate all that has just happened to you.

— Pause.

— When you are ready, let the image of the garden fade and become aware of your breathing. Become aware of your body and the place in which you are meditating, and open your eyes.

Meditation diary

I pictured Mercury in the form of a young man wearing the traditional winged helmet and winged shoes. We got on well together, but I was rather dismayed to find that he had brought a lot of sheep with him which over-ran the garden. I was worried about the damage that they might cause. Mercury told me they were like thoughts — one followed another, and the only way to break a thought pattern was literally to stop thoughts from following one another automatically and to keep them apart. After this the sheep simply disappeared.

Mercury's gift to me was an orange, which he said was to remind me that you have to peel away the skin before it is possible to find something really worthwhile. I wasn't sure what this was to be applied to – Mercury said it could be applied to anything, but he was still talking about thought processes. I took this as a reminder that to achieve anything worthwhile means working at it and peeling off the surface layer to get at the fruit beneath.

VENUS
20 minutes

Venus (Aphrodite to the Greeks) represents our ability to form personal relationships and to bond in a loving way. Personal magnetism comes from the Venus part of personality. Venus also has much to do with social graces and the ability to put a value on things – not in a material sense, however, but in value judgements of likes and dislikes. Venus gives us our sense of interdependence and our ability to cooperate with other people. Basically, Venus in us is the urge and power to attract both people (especially in sexual relationships) and those things which make life fulfilling. The positive qualities of Venus are loving, caring, diplomatic, fruitful, sympathetic and artistic. The negative qualities are promiscuous, materialistic, shallow, hedonistic and self-indulgent.

Mythologically, she is the personification of beauty, for which she loves to be worshipped, and the bounteous giver of life's gifts and pleasures. She represents the divine in nature and is a significant factor in all that is youthfully female or feminine. In Greek mythology Aphrodite was married to Hephaestos, the lame blacksmith god, who forged thunderbolts for Zeus. She was not faithful, however. She is the mother of Eros (in Roman mythology, Cupid).

– Relaxation sequence (page 25).

– Imagine that you are in a garden (see the Inner Garden on page 46). This is not a garden that you know in your outer life, but one that you create in your imagination. Really be there, looking at any flowers, shrubs or trees that may be growing. The garden is enclosed by a high wall. Spend a little time getting to know the garden.

— Pause.

— In the garden there is a particular place with a special atmosphere, a focal point to which you are drawn. Go to this place. Look around you and sense the atmosphere.

— Pause.

— This is a protected place, where no one and nothing may enter without your permission.

— Pause.

— Imagine that you invite Venus into your garden. Imagine that Venus comes to you as a person.

— Pause.

— Build up a picture in your mind of Venus as a person. What is Venus wearing? What does Venus look like?

— Pause.

— How is Venus responding to you, and how do you feel about or react to Venus?

— Pause.

— Spend a little time building up an image of Venus. Take whatever comes to you, and allow the image to change and grow if it wishes to do so.

— Pause.

— Imagine that you greet Venus and begin to talk together. What does Venus want to say to you?

— Pause.

— Spend time getting to know Venus's personality. What qualities and special powers does Venus have?

— Pause.

— Ask Venus to give you a gift or symbol, something that represents your need from Venus. Take whatever occurs to you first, and ask Venus to explain the meaning of the gift.

— Pause.

— What should you do with the gift, and how should you use it?

— Pause.

— Is there anything else that Venus would like to say to you or show you — particularly about the way that you form and conduct your personal relationships?

— Pause.

— When you are ready, thank Venus for being with you and then let the image fade until you are alone again in the garden.

— Pause.

— Contemplate all that has just happened to you.

— Pause.

— When you are ready, let the image of the garden fade and become aware of your breathing. Become aware of your

body and the place in which you are meditating, and open
your eyes.

Meditation diary

I found it difficult at first to get in touch with Venus, or to get
an image of her. Everything kept swirling around. I felt her
presence, and then couldn't seem to stop myself from spiral-
ling around where I sensed her to be. Then suddenly I was
high up in the air looking down on the garden below. I could
see for miles over the surrounding countryside. Then I came
back down to the garden and found Venus waiting there.

She gave me a very heavy metal ball, which I thought at
first was an orange like the one in the Mercury meditation,
but it wasn't. The ball was a dark coppery colour and too
heavy to hold for long. I asked her what it was for, but all she
said was that I ought to 'lighten up'. Then I got a lecture
about how life was not all suffering, as the Buddhists teach,
but that nature and the forces of life could play too, and enjoy
themselves. There are two sides to everything, and Venus told
me that I should not focus too one-sidedly on the heavy side
of life. The ball would become lighter as I did.

Then the garden seemed full of swirling coloured mists, red
and yellow in particular. I was alone again and finished the
meditation.

MARS
20 minutes

Mars (in Greek mythology, Ares) represents aggression,
physical energy and drive. It is the aspect of personality that
evokes the 'fight or flight' response to dangerous or stressful
situations. When manifested positively Mars is dynamic,
active, assertive,enthusiastic and passionate. Negatively, Mars
can be wilful, destructive, overbearing and uncaring.

The Roman Mars was highly venerated. He sired the founders of Rome and was not just a god of war but was also associated with fertility. His aggressive masculine qualities were regarded as being honourable and virtuous. To the Greeks, however, Ares was equated with blind courage, bloody rage and carnage – a brutish bully. Zeus hated him, probably because his wife, Hera, gave birth to him without recourse to Zeus. Mars is the product of Hera's stored up rage – he is *our* stored up anger.

– Relaxation sequence (page 25).

– Imagine that you are in a garden (see the Inner Garden on page 46). This is not a garden that you know in your outer life, but one that you create in your imagination. Really be there, looking at any flowers, shrubs or trees that may be growing. The garden is enclosed by a high wall. Spend a little time getting to know the garden.

– Pause.

– In the garden there is a particular place with a special atmosphere, a focal point to which you are drawn. Go to this place. Look around you and sense the atmosphere.

– Pause.

– This is a protected place, where no one and nothing may enter without your permission.

– Pause.

– Imagine that you invite Mars into your garden. Imagine that Mars comes to you as a person.

– Pause.

– Build up a picture in your mind of Mars as a person. What is Mars wearing? What does Mars look like?

— Pause.

— How is Mars responding to you, and how do you feel about or react to Mars?

— Pause.

— Spend a little time building up an image of Mars. Take whatever comes to you, and allow the image to change and grow if it wishes to do so.

— Pause.

— Imagine that you greet Mars and begin to talk together. What does Mars want to say to you?

— Pause.

— Spend time getting to know Mars's personality. What qualities and special powers does Mars have?

— Pause.

— Ask Mars to give you a gift or symbol, something that represents your need from Mars. Take whatever occurs to you first, and ask Mars to explain the meaning of the gift.

— Pause.

— What should you do with the gift, and how should you use it?

— Pause.

— Is there anything else that Mars would like to say to you or show you — particularly about the way that you should direct your energy and enthusiasm?

— Pause.

— When you are ready, thank Mars for being with you and then let the image fade until you are alone again in the garden.

— Pause.

— Contemplate all that has just happened to you.

— Pause.

— When you are ready, let the image of the garden fade and become aware of your breathing. Become aware of your body and the place in which you are meditating, and open your eyes.

Meditation diary

Mars was a complete surprise to me. I was expecting to picture someone brash, young and aggressive, but instead my imagination created an old man! He was certainly quite physically fit, but well past the years of youthful virility! He said he was tired of being aggressive and just wanted to enjoy life a little now and at a slow pace too. No more wars. Mars said he would enjoy my company for a while and would welcome the chance to talk. He gave me a silver star to wear on my forehead (I took this to be a symbol of foresight), saying that growing old was not something to be feared nor something which meant the loss of physical beauty. Rather the opposite. I accepted the gift and said that I would return to meet him again soon. Then I ended the meditation.

JUPITER
20 minutes

Jupiter (in Greek mythology, Zeus) represents growth and expansion, the ability to assimilate experience and turn this into maturing wisdom. Jupiter is one's conscience, and when expressed positively is wise, philosophical, easy-going, sociable, opportunistic, future-oriented, enriching and generous. However, if expressed negatively Jupiter becomes self-indulgent, over-exuberant, self-righteous and hypo-critical.

In mythology, Jupiter/Zeus was the very powerful, all-pervading father god. What he could not take by persuasion he would take by force, wielding his thunderbolts in the process. Able to change his form, Jupiter has a connection with prophets and seers, thus associating him with the arche-typal shaman figure, the person who can move at will between this world and the dimensions of spiritual reality. Thus in mythology, Jupiter ruled over both the earth (physical world) and the sky (the spiritual world).

— Relaxation sequence (page 25).

— Imagine that you are in a garden (see the Inner Garden on page 46). This is not a garden that you know in your outer life, but one that you create in your imagination. Really be there, looking at any flowers, shrubs or trees that may be growing. The garden is enclosed by a high wall. Spend a little time getting to know the garden.

— Pause.

— In the garden there is a particular place with a special atmosphere, a focal point to which you are drawn. Go to this place. Look around you and sense the atmosphere.

— Pause.

— This is a protected place, where no one and nothing may enter without your permission.

— Pause.

– Imagine that you invite Jupiter into your garden. Imagine that Jupiter comes to you as a person.

– Pause.

– Build up a picture in your mind of Jupiter as a person. What is Jupiter wearing? What does Jupiter look like?

– Pause.

– How is Jupiter responding to you, and how do you feel about or react to Jupiter?

– Pause.

– Spend a little time building up an image of Jupiter. Take whatever comes to you, and allow the image to change and grow if it wishes to do so.

– Pause.

– Imagine that you greet Jupiter and begin to talk together. What does Jupiter want to say to you?

– Pause.

– Spend time getting to know Jupiter's personality. What qualities and special powers does Jupiter have?

– Pause.

– Ask Jupiter to give you a gift or symbol, something that represents your need from Jupiter. Take whatever occurs to you first, and ask Jupiter to explain the meaning of the gift.

– Pause.

— What should you do with the gift, and how should you use it?

— Pause.

— Is there anything else that Jupiter would like to say to you or show you — particularly about the way that you can grow, develop and increase your experience in the future?

— Pause.

— When you are ready, thank Jupiter for being with you and then let the image fade until you are alone again in the garden.

— Pause.

— Contemplate all that has just happened to you.

— Pause.

— When you are ready, let the image of the garden fade and become aware of your breathing. Become aware of your body and the place in which you are meditating, and open your eyes.

Meditation diary

The garden seemed quite dark this time — I saw it at dusk, as it was in the moon meditation. I spent some time wandering around and also feeling things. I picked up some old leaves and crumbled them between my fingers, feeling the texture. I also ran my fingers along a hedge, feeling how prickly it was. Everything seemed very real and solid. I became aware of a figure standing a little way away from me. As I focused my attention on it, it became clearer. The figure looked like a cross between someone in a spacesuit and the tin man in *The Wizard of Oz*. This was Jupiter. As I approached the figure seemed to become much bigger and taller – or perhaps I became smaller. The figure picked me up and cradled me like a baby. I was quite surprised to discover that Jupiter was a woman. Jupiter explained that 'he' could adopt any form he wished. He unbuttoned his tunic and I saw that inside there was no body – nothing in fact. Jupiter could not be seen unless clothed in some form or other, in this case a spacesuit.

I asked Jupiter for a gift, but he didn't seem to want to give me anything. Then he asked me what I would like and I said the gift of foresight and prophecy, knowing that these came within Jupiter's sphere. I don't know if I received anything or not, because Jupiter faded from the scene at that point and left me alone again.

SATURN
20 minutes

Saturn (in Greek mythology, Cronos) who represents authority, the law and social responsibility, usually gets quite a bad press. However, the idea is to learn about one's personal limitations and then to be able to work within them. Saturn teaches that it's no use aiming for the impossible. When expressed positively through the personality, Saturn is patient, reliable, organised, self-disciplined, dutiful and responsible. Saturn's negative expression is pessimistic, depressive, rigid, mistrustful and even malicious. Saturn is also the archetype which governs such feelings as depression and melancholy, so if you are feeling depressed it is Saturn at work and in need of attention.

To the Greeks, Cronos was a destructive god of time, but in Rome his equivalent, Saturn, ruled over a Golden Age.

– Relaxation sequence (page 25).

– Imagine that you are in a garden (see the Inner Garden, on page 46). This is not a garden that you know in your outer life, but one that you create in your imagination. Really be there, looking at any flowers, shrubs or trees that may be growing. The garden is enclosed by a high wall. Spend a little time getting to know the garden.

— Pause.

— In the garden there is a particular place with a special atmosphere, a focal point to which you are drawn. Go to this place. Look around you and sense the atmosphere.

— Pause.

— This is a protected place, where no one and nothing may enter without your permission.

— Pause.

— Imagine that you invite Saturn into your garden. Imagine that Saturn comes to you as a person.

— Pause.

— Build up a picture in your mind of Saturn as a person. What is Saturn wearing. What does Saturn look like?

— Pause.

— How is Saturn responding to you, and how do you feel about or react to Saturn?

— Pause.

— Spend a little time building up an image of Saturn. Take whatever comes to you, and allow the image to change and grow if it wishes to do so.

— Pause.

– Imagine that you greet Saturn and begin to talk together. What does Saturn want to say to you?

– Pause.

– Spend time getting to know Saturn's personality. What qualities and special powers does Saturn have?

– Pause.

– Ask Saturn to give you a gift or symbol, something that represents your need from Saturn. Take whatever occurs to you first, and ask Saturn to explain the meaning of the gift.

– Pause.

– What should you do with the gift, and how should you use it?

– Pause.

– Is there anything else that Saturn would like to say to you or show you – particularly about your responsibilities and the tasks which you should do?

– Pause.

– When you are ready, thank Saturn for being with you and then let the image fade until you are alone again in the garden.

– Pause.

– Contemplate all that has just happened to you.

– Pause.

– When you are ready, let the image of the garden fade and become aware of your breathing. Become aware of your body and the place in which you are meditating, and open your eyes.

Meditation diary

As much as I wanted to go to the garden, the image of a forest clearing came strongly to me. There I met a knight on horseback who took me up on his horse and away through the trees. We came to a castle and the knight left me, telling me to enter. I did, and was shown to a stable which was to be my quarters. Then Saturn came to me. He was an old man with long white hair, wearing white robes, and was apparently the king of the castle. He didn't seem very pleased to see me and wanted to be left alone. However, I persuaded him to give me a gift which was a silver orb, a sign, he said, of the 'way of the world'. Saturn told me that I should play my role with more commitment. I asked him if he was the Grail King and he laughed and said no. I think he may have been. . . .

THE SUN
20 minutes

The sun represents the inner self, and it is the energy which integrates all the different qualities of your personality to make you a whole person. The sun regulates and maintains equilibrium, so if there is a sense of imbalance in your life it is the sun that you should approach in your meditation. The sun also has much to do with strength of will – the ability to achieve your ambitions and desires. Positively expressed, the sun is self-assured, independent and creative; negatively, the sun expresses egotism, incompetence and aggression.

Mythologically, sun gods are always an important part of the pantheon; the Greek sun god Apollo is a well-known example. The sun forms a pair with the moon, representing masculine extroverted forces of consciousness as opposed to the moon's feminine, introverted rulership of the inner worlds and the unconscious.

— Relaxation sequence (page 25).

— Imagine that you are in a garden (see the Inner Garden on page 46). This is not a garden that you know in your outer life, but one that you create in your imagination. Really be there, looking at any flowers, shrubs or trees that may be growing. The garden is enclosed by a high wall. Spend a little time getting to know the garden.

— Pause.

— In the garden there is a particular place with a special atmosphere, a focal point to which you are drawn. Go to this place. Look around you and sense the atmosphere.

— Pause.

— This is a protected place, where no one and nothing may enter without your permission.

— Pause.

— Imagine that you invite the sun into your garden. Imagine that the sun comes to you as a person.

— Pause.

— Build up a picture in your mind of the sun as a person. What is the sun wearing? What does the sun look like?

— Pause.

— How is the sun responding to you and how do you feel about or react to the sun?

— Pause.

— Spend a little time building up an image of the sun. Take whatever comes to you and allow the image to change and grow if it wishes to do so.

— Pause.

— Imagine that you greet the sun and begin to talk together. What does the sun want to say to you?

— Pause.

— Spend time getting to know the sun's personality. What qualities and special powers does the sun have?

— Pause.

— Ask the sun to give you a gift or symbol, something that represents your need from the sun. Take whatever occurs to you first, and ask the sun to explain the meaning of the gift.

— Pause.

— What should you do with the gift, and how should you use it?

— Pause.

— Is there anything else that the sun would like to say to you or show you — particularly about developing a sense of purpose in your life?

— Pause.

— When you are ready, thank the sun for being with you and then let the image fade until you are alone again in the garden.

– Pause.

– Contemplate all that has just happened to you.

– Pause.

– When you are ready, let the image of the garden fade and become aware of your breathing. Become aware of your body and the place in which you are meditating, and open your eyes.

Meditation diary

For me, this meditation was quite short but to the point. The sun appeared as a North American Indian who stayed long enough to tell me that, although the sun was a symbol of the Great Spirit, it was much more than this and represented something which suggested the wholeness and oneness of all life. The sun told me that his rays could burn or nurture, and to help me understand gave me a pair of 'Reactolite' sunglasses – the type that go darker as the light gets brighter. With a warning not to look directly at the sun, he was off again.

I spent some time alone in the garden going over this experience – although the sun had only been with me for a short while, I felt that the experience was significant for me and that it was worth spending time letting its meaning unfold and become clearer. The colours in the garden seemed very beautiful, especially the green of grass and leaves which were almost luminescent.

This concludes the meditations in this chapter, and also concludes all the principal meditations. Chapters 8 and 9 include food for thought and inspiration that you can introduce into your meditations to deepen your experience.

8

MEDITATIONS FOR INSIGHT AND INSPIRATION

Quotations for Meditation

From the inspiring quotations which follow, choose one that is appropriate for you. Then memorise it, or write it down on a piece of card. You can use your quotation in a meditation, contemplating its meaning. Alternatively, you could carry the card with you to inspire you through the day, or leave it propped up in a visible place at home or at work.

A tree that can fill the span of a man's arms grows from a
  downy tip;
A terrace nine storeys high rises from hodfuls of earth;
A journey of a thousand miles starts from beneath one's feet.

LAO-TZU

It is not because things are difficult that we do not dare; it is because we do not dare that they are difficult.

SENECA

Imagination is more important than knowledge.

ALBERT EINSTEIN

e from the unreal to the real.
ne from darkness to light.
me from death to immortality.

Upanishads

To know yet to think that one does not know is best;
Not to know yet to think that one knows will lead to difficulty.

LAO TZU

Go placidly amid the noise and haste, and remember what
peace there may be in silence.

DESIDERATA

Ask, and it will be given you; seek and you will find; knock,
and it will be opened to you.

BIBLE, MATTHEW 7:7

There is a feeling that a new type of man has been emerging in
the past two hundred years and that the human race is now
ready for an evolutionary leap.

COLIN WILSON

It is the soul that sees; the outward eyes
Present the object; but the mind descries.

GEORGE CRABBE

Inner peace can be reached only when we practise forgiveness. Forgiveness is the letting go of the past, and is
therefore the means for correcting our misperceptions.

GERALD JAMPOLSKY

When a man surrenders all desires that come to the heart and
by the grace of God finds the joy of God, then his soul has
indeed found peace.

Bhagavad Gita

Life was never meant to be a struggle, just a gentle progression from one point to another, much like walking through a
valley on a sunny day.

STUART WILDE

Begin difficult things while they are easy,
do great things while they are small.
The difficult things of the world
must once have been easy;
The great things must once have been small. . . .
A thousand-mile journey begins with one step.

LAO-TZU

What is life? It is the flash of a firefly in the night. It is the breath of a buffalo in the wintertime. It is the little shadow which runs across the grass and loses itself in the sunset.

CROWFOOT

Yoga is the settling of the mind into silence. When the mind has settled, we are established in our essential nature, which is unbounded consciousness.

PATANJALI

The old sense of sinfulness has given way to an acknowledgment of unfulfilled potential and separation from God is now seen as illusion to be dispelled through a realisation of true identity.

PETER SPINK

If you are still being hurt by an event that happened to you at twelve, it is the thought that is hurting you now.

JAMES HILLMAN

And this our life, exempt from public haunt,
Finds tongues in trees, books in running brooks,
Sermons in stones and good in everything.

WILLIAM SHAKESPEARE

When you affirm your rightness in the universe, then you cooperate with others easily and automatically as part of your own nature. You, being yourself, help others be themselves.

JANE ROBERTS

Be gentle with yourself. If you will not be your own unconditional friend, who will be? If you are playing an opponent and you are also opposing yourself – you are going to be outnumbered.

DAN MILLMAN

To perceive a distant reality as real is the function of imagination. The words 'perception' and 'imagination' become interchangeable on this level.

COLIN WILSON

Don't be afraid to take a big step if one is indicated. You can't cross a chasm in two small jumps.

DAVID LLOYD GEORGE

Danger itself
Fosters the rescuing power.

FRIEDRICH HÖLDERLIN

That thou mayest have pleasure in everything, seek pleasure in nothing.
That thou mayest know everything seek to know nothing.
That thou mayest possess all things, seek to possess nothing.
That thou mayest be everything, seek to be nothing.

ST JOHN OF THE CROSS

Those who know do not talk.

LAO TZU

Consciousness consists primarily of what we know, and what we know we know.

JUNE SINGER

Earth's crammed with heaven
And every common bush afire with God.

ELIZABETH BARRETT BROWNING

We must admit that what is closest to us is the very thing we know least about, although it seems to be what we know best of all.

CARL JUNG

Live and work but do not forget to play, to have fun in life and really enjoy it.

EILEEN CADDY

I learned that nothing is impossible when we follow our inner guidance, even when its direction may threaten us by reversing our usual logic.

GERALD JAMPOLSKY

I have learned more from my mistakes than from my successes.

SIR HUMPHRY DAVY

When we forgive someone, the knots are untied and the past is released.

RESHAD FEILD

Silence is the element in which great things fashion themselves.

THOMAS CARLYLE

Every person, all the events of your life are there because you have drawn them there.

RICHARD BACH

Love alone can unite living beings so as to complete and fulfil them . . . for it alone joins them by what is deepest in themselves. All we need is to imagine our ability to love developing until it embraces the totality of men and of the earth.

TEILHARD DE CHARDIN

Fate and soul are two names for the same principle.

NOVALIS

In a world where death is the hunter, my friend, there is no time for regrets or doubts. There is only time for decisions.

CARLOS CASTANEDA

Good ideas and innovations must be driven into existence by courageous patience.

HYMAN RICKOVER

I never saw a moor
I never saw the sea;
Yet I know how the
heather looks
And what a wave must be.

EMILY DICKINSON

The owl whose night-bound eyes are blind unto the day cannot unveil the mystery of light. If you would indeed behold the spirit of death, open your heart wide unto the body of life. For life and death are one, even as the river and the sea are one.

KAHLIL GIBRAN

Death cannot kill what never dies.

WILLIAM PENN

There is a time to keep silent and a time to speak.

BIBLE, ECCLESIASTES 3:7

'To be or not to be' is not the question; it is the answer.

FRED ALAN WOLF

Only in relationship can you know yourself, not in abstraction and certainly not in isolation.

J. KRISHNAMURTI

In all activities of life from trivial to important the secret of efficiency lies in an ability to combine two seemingly incompatible states – a state of maximum activity and a state of maximum relaxation.

ALDOUS HUXLEY

Utterly impossible as are all these events they are probably as like those which may have taken place as any others which never took person at all are ever likely to be.

JAMES JOYCE

To know how to wait is the great secret of success.

JOSEPHE DE MAISTRE

Life is eternal; and love is immortal; and death is only a horizon; and a horizon is nothing save the limit of our sight.

ROSSITER WORTHINGTON RAYMOND

Love seeketh not itself to please,
Nor for itself hath any care,
But for another gives its ease,
And builds a Heaven in Hell's despair.

WILLIAM BLAKE

The superior work you have done so industriously in quietness should be applied when you are submerged in the tumult of your daily life.

GARMA CHANG

The most effective way to achieve right relations with any living thing is to look for the best in it, and then help that best into the fullest expression.

J. ALLEN BOONE

The Lord is in me, the Lord is in you, as life is in every seed.

KABIR

Simplicity is the highest quality of expression. It is that quality to which art comes in its supreme moments. It makes the final stage of growth. It is the rarest, as it is the most precious result which men secure in their self-training.

LAO TZU

Accept with love the flaws of your friends and enemies, and you may learn to love and accept yourself.

RESHAD FEILD

A step in the wrong direction is better than staying on the spot all your life. Once you've moving forward you can correct your course as you go. Your automatic guidance system cannot guide you when you're standing still.

MAXWELL MALTZ

When you reach the centre of Consciousness, you find a complete stillness — a deep well of silence. It is not power, since there is nothing for it to be a power to, or over. It just *is*.

JOEL GOLDSMITH

You are given the gifts of the gods; you create your reality according to your beliefs. Yours is the creative energy that makes your world. There are no limitations to the self except those you believe in.

JANE ROBERTS

It is eternity now.
I am in the midst of it.
    It is about me
    in the sunshine;
I am in it,
as the butterfly floats
in the light-laden air.
Nothing has to come;
    it is now.
Now is eternity;
now is the immortal life.

RICHARD JEFFERIES

We grow great by dreams. All big men are dreamers. They see things in the soft haze of a spring day or in the red fire of a long winter's evening. Some of us let our dreams die, but others nourish and protect them, nurse them through bad days till they bring them to sunshine and light.

WOODROW WILSON

Let my love, like sunlight, surround you and yet give you illumined freedom.

RABINDRANATH TAGORE

The way you activate the seeds of your creation is by making choices about the results you want to create. When you make a choice, you mobilise vast human energies and resources which otherwise go untapped.

ROBERT FRITZ

Where can I find a man who has forgotten words? He is the one I would like to talk to.

CHUANG TSU

There is only one courage and that is the courage to go on dying to the past, not to collect it, not to accumulate it, not to cling to it. We all cling to the past, and because we cling to the past we become unavailable to the present.

BHAGWAN SHREE RAJNEESH

Flow with the rhythm of nature. Blend with all there is around you.

EILEEN CADDY

Sometimes the only way for me to find out what it is I want to do is go ahead and do something. Then the moment I start to act, my feelings become clear.

HUGH PRATHER

To every thing there is a season, and a time to every purpose under the heaven:

A time to be born, and a time to die; a time to plant, and a time to pluck up that which is planted;
A time to weep, and a time to laugh; a time to mourn and a time to dance.

BIBLE, ECCLESIASTES 3:1

Many people sit around waiting for the world to discover them, and that rarely happens. If you move toward your goals, expressing all your power, opportunity will find you as a result of your actions.

STUART WILDE

In every human being there slumber faculties by means of which he can acquire for himself a knowledge of higher worlds.

RUDOLF STEINER

Do your best quietly and you will be working in accordance with that divine law which will 'make crooked places straight', and restore harmony and health.

WHITE EAGLE

Our chief want in life is somebody who shall make us do what we can.

RALPH WALDO EMERSON

Feel the fear. . . . And do it anyway.

SUSAN JEFFERS

Humankind learns much faster through adversity. If everything is easy and no obstacle is in our way we never learn anything.

ELISABETH KÜBLER-ROSS

Take rest; a field that has rested gives a beautiful crop.

OVID

To re-align ourselves with energy requires a complete stilling of our habitual response to external and internal stimuli.

LAWRENCE BLAIR

When love beckons to you, follow him.
Though his ways are hard and steep.
And when his wings enfold you, yield to him.
Though the sword hidden among his pinions may wound you.

KAHLIL GIBRAN

Humour is the great thing, the saving thing after all. The minute it crops up, all our hardnesses yield, all our irritations and resentments slip away and a sunny spirit takes their place.

MARK TWAIN

The reasons why birds can fly and we can't is simply that they have perfect faith, for to have faith is to have wings.

J. M. BARRIE

You get what you need, you always get what you need, you don't always get what you want.

ELISABETH KÜBLER-ROSS

A lot of successful people are risk-takers. Unless you're willing to do that — to have a go, fail miserably, and have another go — success won't happen.

PHILLIP ADAMS

One day, the master's pupil came to him after months of practising meditation in a state of great excitement. 'I have just seen the Buddha in my meditation,' he said, expecting great praise from his teacher. 'Never mind,' the sage replied, 'Go back and try again. With a bit of luck he will have gone away now.'

ZEN ANECDOTE

9

MEDITATIONS
FOR EVERY DAY
OF YOUR LIFE

This chapter will help you to face and cope with difficult or negative qualities and emotions, either in yourself or encountered in other people. Then, to balance these negative situations, I have included a selection of ideas for meditations that are aimed at nurturing positive experiences in your life. There are fifty-two, which gives one for each week of the year if that is how you decide to use them.

From the following list select the experience that you want to meditate on, and then find the appropriate short text later in the chapter. Use the relaxation technique to enter meditation and then make your chosen text the basis for meditation. You can use them in conjunction with other meditations already described, or they can stand on their own as a focal point for contemplation.

You might like to write down your chosen text on a card to carry with you during the day, or, at home or at work, prop it up close to you so that you can contemplate its meaning as you go about your daily activities. And you could pass a second card on to someone who you feel may be in need of support and could benefit from a particular idea or meditation.

Another method is to let fate choose for you. When you want to choose a paragraph, close your eyes and think of a number between one and fifty-two. Let the meditation bearing that number be your choice.

The first section is to do with dealing with negative experiences. Choose the one most relevant to you and then choose the corresponding meditation notes which will encourage positive experiences, so as to balance negative and positive. To achieve a balance is important. Don't dwell too much on the negative aspects of life, as many people tend to do, but balance this up with a positive approach.

However, some people go to the opposite extreme and consider only the positive aspects of life. This is not right, for we all contain the potential for negative emotions and thoughts, and if these are constantly denied or suppressed they continue to work on us unconsciously, intensifying rather than disappearing. If we deny our own negative side, one result is that our negativity appears outside us – we see it in other people, who then become carriers of our own problems and difficulties. You can spot this most easily when you encounter someone in whom you have great difficulty finding any positive qualities!

Dealing with Negative Experiences

1. Anxiety
2. Depression
3. Loss of confidence
4. Guilt
5. Self-loathing
6. Weakness
7. Sadness
8. Hurt or pain
9. Disappointment
10. Worry
11. Hatred
12. Fear

13. Loneliness
14. Selfishness
15. Thoughtlessness
16. Greed
17. Dishonesty
18. Jealousy
19. Cruelty
20. Destructiveness
21. Despair
22. Exhaustion
23. Anger
24. Confusion
25. Failure
26. Bitterness

SUGGESTIONS FOR MEDITATION
1 ANXIETY

People suffer anxiety when anticipating that something negative may happen to them in the future. But why be anxious about something that may never happen? Let your thoughts dwell on the present, not on the future. The future may never come, but the present is always here and should be experienced to the full. Being anxious means that you are missing out on what is happening here and now. You are denying your existence at this moment of time. Live in the present moment, enjoying life as it happens to you. So don't be anxious about life as it *may* happen. The here and now is all that matters. The here and now *is* happening.

2
DEPRESSION

A state of depression may seem to be a never-ending experience, a hole into which you have fallen and cannot climb out.

Perhaps you cannot do so at this moment in time, but remember that your depression is a sign that something is trying to be born – something new and exciting. The birth is difficult and oppressive, but if you will let this intelligent process be, you will discover that your depression is leading to new possibilities. You are travelling through a dark tunnel and cannot yet see the light at the end. You are moving forward through time, and that light will eventually come. Don't dwell on the depression, but prepare yourself for the future light. Heighten your sensitivity to what is going on in you that has not yet come into the light of your consciousness. Depression is a phase, not a condition. It will pass.

3
LOSS OF CONFIDENCE

Having no confidence means that you are out of touch with your inner strength and resources. Forget what others think of you, what others might say if you fail. You owe it to yourself to let your inner strength support you. That is what it is there for. Don't stand in your own way; no one else is doing so. It is not other people who are preventing you from doing what you wish to do, but you yourself. Contemplate this idea and find the source of your inner strength and confidence. It is there – we all have it. We all have the ability to draw on an inner well-spring of support which is endless in its power and strength. Your task is to find it and then give it free expression.

4
GUILT

If you are feeling guilty, you must *do* something. Guilt encourages passivity and eats up your energy, your life. If you have done something that you regret, don't ponder on it any longer but act to redeem yourself. The experience of guilt usually involves another person. You must go to that person and tell them how you feel in order to resolve the situation. When you meditate on this you may find that it is fear that is preventing you from dealing with your guilt. If so, your problem is not guilt but fear (see 12). Don't allow the guilt to fester, but express it. If your guilt is directed solely at yourself and does not involve anyone else, the solution is simple. In meditation you must talk through your guilt with yourself, admit it to yourself, and then be kind to yourself.

5
SELF-LOATHING

This state is the result of not living up to your own standards, of failing to be something that you are not and perhaps can never be. But are these really your standards? Are they perhaps somebody else's? Or are they standards that you have never questioned but accepted for as long as you can remember? You must check this out – are the standards you set for yourself the right ones and do you really want them? If you could start again, what would be the standards that you really set for yourself? Don't think about other people; think about yourself. We all have qualities and experiences in common, but every human being is also an individual. If you experience self-loathing you must meditate not on those things that you have in common with others, but on the differences, the things that make you what you are, and you should honour those differences.

6
WEAKNESS

If you are experiencing weakness it is because you are comparing your strength with something that is much stronger than you. Perhaps it is time to accept exactly what you are and who you are, and that includes your weaknesses. By accepting them you will become strong, not in a relative sense but in the way that you experience yourself. This is what is meant by inner strength, which owes nothing to comparison with the strength of others. Accept yourself and grow strong inwardly.

7
SADNESS

The experience of sadness is an important one for human beings. You have known something or someone wonderful, or perhaps had an experience that has now come to an end; nevertheless you have had that privilege, and no one can take its memory away from you. You may not be able to repeat the experience, but the fact that the memory lives inside you means that somewhere in your consciousness it is still real and will continue to be with you for all time. Sadness means that somewhere inside you lies the experience of a precious time that has now gone by. Even though it has gone, the present moment contains its special qualities for which you should give thanks. Thank your good fortune that you are sad!

8
HURT OR PAIN

If you are experiencing hurt or pain, be aware of the compassion that exists in the world. Compassion means that others are aware of the meaning and experience of suffering and are feeling for you. Feel supported by the compassion that truly exists in the world in endless supply. Human suffering seems great and endless, but so too is compassion; and although you may feel alone in your suffering, others have been there before you and will come after you. The way that you bear your hurt or pain will add to the compassion in the world and its support for those that come after you. Your experience of hurt or pain means that you now know exactly what others will feel too; and you can therefore lend them true support based on a compassion born out of personal pain.

9
DISAPPOINTMENT

This too is good! It means that you wanted something badly enough to feel disappointment when you could not have it. Enriched now by all that you have learnt, turn away from your failure and face the future squarely. Make your battle plans carefully, leaving nothing unconsidered. Now is the moment of decision, and the decision must be to go on, to try again. When success comes you will feel it all the more keenly, for you know now what disappointment means. Don't waste the experience, but use it as a driving force that takes you on towards your goal.

10
WORRY

What a many-headed thought monster worry is – cut off one head and two more grow in its place! It is in the night that the worry monster is at its most powerful. Consider this: when you have a worrying thought, combat it with a positive thought. Think about those things that you love in life, that you value most. Don't wait for the monster to strike, but prepare your positive thoughts now. Get them ready before the battle. It's no good mustering unprepared defences in the night. Get them ready in advance, during the friendly time of the day, while the monster sleeps. When worry strikes, bring out your postive thoughts and you will find that the monster dissolves.

11
HATRED

This is a strong emotion, and if you feel an emotion strongly enough it can point to something that lies hidden inside yourself. Perhaps you have just cause to feel this way. Even though the object of your hatred may be deserving there is the possibility that what you hate in others is something that lives in yourself – a part of yourself that you have failed to recognise and that festers away through the feeling of hatred. The world is full of 'others' who are wrong where we are right; 'others' who have done bad, while we are always good. Maturity and experience teach us that the world is not black and white like this, that each human being has a black as well as a white side, although the dark, unlived side is usually hidden from public view. Find this side in yourself and contemplate it. If you can acknowledge it, your hate will be transformed. No longer will you be eaten alive by it, and no longer will you have enemies.

12
FEAR

This feeling is a dragon that must be faced and conquered. One way is to think of the worst thing that could possibly happen to you in your given circumstances. Contemplate these things one by one and look at them from all angles. Make sure you know everything about these worst possible things. You will realise that, whatever happens, it won't be any worse than that. If you do this properly you will find your fear turning to elation at the thought of going into battle with your dragon, and when you have defeated it you will release something beautiful within yourself: a hidden treasure will be found.

13
LONELINESS

Being unable to share ourselves and our experiences with another person brings loneliness. If you experience loneliness, turn inwards and be company for the many facets of your own inner world. You will find your loneliness dispelled and your world populated with so many new and unexplored facets that you will forget your problem. Even more, you will discover that you are living in a world that is alive and a world with which you do have a relationship. You are not alone after all, but can make friends wherever you look. If after all this you want to share this living world within with another person – if you want a friend – then you have to be a friend yourself. Don't wait for the world to come to you, but go out and look for it.

14
SELFISHNESS

Loneliness and selfishness have much in common and feed off one another. Keeping something for yourself and not sharing it with others means that you cut yourself off from the world and from potential relationships with others. Selfishness is the breeding ground of loneliness. When you treat others in a certain way, or when you treat yourself in a certain way, the response tends to be complementary. In other words, if others seem selfish it is in response to your own selfish qualities. Go out and do a deliberately generous thing, and the world will respond accordingly. A random act of kindness is called for here.

15
THOUGHTLESSNESS

Meditation is often said to be a selfish, self-centred thing. It is accused of being thoughtless, not in the sense of having no thought (for this is sometimes a quality of meditation) but in the sense of having no concern for others. You, on the other hand, may see that thoughtlessness in the sense of having no concern for others can come about through *lack* of meditation, through not spending a little time being aware, stopping and being sensitive to the messages that are trying to get through to you. A thoughtless person might benefit from being still for a while, contemplating all that is going on and in particular contemplating the needs of others.

16
GREED

Be aware of where your limits should lie, especially when you are accumulating something. Going beyond those limits means that your gain is someone else's loss, and there is a natural line over which you should not go. Indeed, stepping over the line means that your gains are not true gains — in some other department you will be losing. For example, greed for possessions leads to a loss of the sense of the true value of life. If you value things more than people then you may have succumbed to greed. If on the list of your priorities material gain is more important than the health of yourself and your friends, your future path may be a difficult one. Find your line, your natural limit, and work within it. Then you will have time for all the things in life that really matter.

17
DISHONESTY

If there is dishonesty in your life then meditate on it, find out where it comes from and why it is there. Then determine exactly who you are being dishonest with. Perhaps it is with yourself; perhaps you have not been entirely honest with yourself about what you want from life, about what you should and shouldn't do. If this is the case, you are standing in your own way and can make no further progress. Remember the Emperor's New Clothes — there is nothing to be gained by dishonesty even if you are going along with the crowd. Be your own person and be true to yourself, and then you will see clearly what it is that you must do.

18
JEALOUSY

Being jealous is to deny yourself. It is, on a simple level, to wish that you were someone else, wishing you had what they have. This is wishing your own life away; it is wishing away the most precious thing that has been given to you. If you find others are jealous of you, do not treat it as a compliment but see if there is some way that you can give away what you have and others want. If you experience jealousy in yourself, first meditate on the object of your desire. Then see yourself as already having it. What you want is not outside yourself, it is in you: you simply haven't discovered it yet. Your jealousy will then disappear.

19
CRUELTY

The natural world is full of cruelty. This is not in itself bad. Cruelty is only bad if it can be avoided. Causing unnecessary and deliberate pain to another being is really what cruelty is all about. If you experience this, either in someone else or in yourself, then meditate on cruelty and look for a missing connection in your life, a connection that has been broken at some time. When that connection is reforged, true feelings and compassion can flow again. You will see how wrong cruelty is, for you will feel what it is like to suffer from cruelty. So first find the break, then mend it. The key will unlock your feelings and they will flow again unhindered. When this happens, don't be afraid to cry for this will be a sign of sincerity.

20
DESTRUCTIVENESS

The urge to destroy is a creative urge under great pressure – blocked or frustrated. Destructiveness can be dealt with by removing an obstacle, whatever that obstacle may be for you. Then destruction can become the basis for creation, the clearing away of the old so that there is room for the new to grow. This process needs some understanding, for destruction is rarely blind – there is usually a motive. Find what the motive is, be clear about what the destructive process is aiming for in the future, then remove any blocks to it and let it transform naturally into creativity.

21
DESPAIR

Perhaps now is the time to let go, to release everything that is causing despair so that you can start anew, not bound in any way to the impossible. Simply let go. If you are experiencing despair, it may be that you are trying to go against the flow, to push the river. If so, change your direction so that you can receive the support of hidden energies. Go with the flow, even if this means an apparent step backwards. You will find yourself taken in a different direction and your despair no longer exists.

22
EXHAUSTION

This is exactly the time when you can turn inwards and receive nourishment to revive your life energies. Don't prevent them coming through. The unconscious is an inexhaustible supply of life's bounties, and you can rest upon it and receive its blessing. It is through our dreams in sleep – or in meditation – that we receive replenishment. A time for renewal has come, so you must find peace within yourself. Something may be sucking away your life energies, so you must find this negative influence and release it. You will find the solution within yourself.

23
ANGER

Don't feel guilty about expressing your anger – it is not good to hold it in. Expressed openly, it will cleanse and release you from its negative effects. So express your anger, but make sure that it is not blind, that you can control it and not cause irreparable harm. Friends and loved ones will understand and support you. Anger stored up and not expressed, however, will eat you up from the inside and eventually come out in an uncontrolled, destructive fashion. It is far better to acknowledge your anger and channel it effectively.

24
CONFUSION

When you cannot make sense of life, when a rational approach to understanding has failed you, that is the time to have faith in your intuition. Don't ask for answers, but look to your feelings. Let them speak for you. Don't try to be logical, but look to the messages that come from the unconscious to your imagination and your dreams. Now is the time to work with your personal symbols and let them work on you. Don't analyse them but simply live with them, allowing them to grow, change and develop. Imagination comes before insight. Intuition comes before the right conclusion. The time of confusion is the night before the day. It is at the beginning of a process, so stay with it and all will become clear.

25
FAILURE

When you see others being successful at something that you would like to achieve, be aware that all you are seeing is the success. Behind this may lie many failures, perhaps even deeper ones than your own. This has not stopped the person from going on to turn their failures into success. All things turn eventually into their opposites. This is the way that situations in life work on the deepest level, and so it is only natural that your failure will turn into success if you see the process through to its natural conclusion.

26
BITTERNESS

The feeling of bitterness is not a pleasant one and yet it is a human feeling and there is a right and wrong way to approach it. Rather like biting into a lemon, the feeling can come as a shock to the system but is one which does not last. And this is the point; bitterness should be felt and then it should pass. If your bitterness lingers, let it go. Don't bite into the same fruit twice. Often mixed with feelings of bitterness are sweet memories, and it is these that you should allow to come to the fore. Meditate on the meaning of bitter-sweet, and you may see how a feeling that is not pleasant can throw into relief its opposite. You cannot live life fully without tasting the full range of human experience.

Nurturing Positive Experiences

27. Love
28. Joy

29. Success
30. Confidence
31. Generosity
32. Support
33. Giving
34. Receiving
35. Anticipation
36. Friendship
37. Longing
38. Hope
39. Dedication
40. Bravery
41. Nurture
42. Selflessness
43. Honesty
44. Wisdom
45. Sensitivity
46. Kindness
47. Endurance
48. Support
49. Solitude
50. Healing
51. Compassion
52. Awareness

SUGGESTIONS FOR MEDITATION
27 LOVE

One of the greatest gifts to humankind is the ability to love. When we enter a loving relationship with someone or something two relationships are formed – one with the outer person and another with an inner person, with a part of ourselves. This is the true sense of healing, to come into relationship and make whole. Hence love is healing on a mundane level, but it works in a cosmic sense too, for it is possible to form a relationship with something much greater at work in the universe. The experience of this 'something much greater' grows with love.

28
JOY

The experience of joy can come from anything when you appreciate it in the right way. Joy comes spontaneously when we open ourselves to it and allow it to enter into our consciousness. It is almost as if it is waiting to be allowed in, and as soon as we open the gate it is there. Joy can be found most easily in small things, if we will only contemplate them: in the colours that meet our eyes and the sounds that meet our ears all through the day. Simply open your eyes and ears and joy can enter in.

29
SUCCESS

Manifesting success is a matter of positive thinking. To be successful, act as if you *are* successful. Be clear about what success means to you. But this does not mean that you have an excuse for doing nothing! You may need to do a lot of work in order to achieve success. Are you pleasing others or pleasing yourself? This also is a question that needs careful consideration, because your idea of what success means is not necessarily the same as other people's. To be truly successful you have to be yourself, to find what freedom means to you and to experience it. First, find what it is that you should be doing. Then do it.

30
CONFIDENCE

Faith and confidence go hand in hand. If there is a task that you need to perform and you want the confidence to do it well, first ensure you are well prepared. Make your plans carefully and attend to all the details. Then forget them and do your task. You will discover that if you have done your groundwork something will come to meet you halfway, will come through you to lend support.

31
GENEROSITY

Being generous is a way of life, not just something that you do. Generosity of spirit means sharing yourself and your gifts with others. Allow yourself to become full of whatever it is you can offer others, then open yourself so that it can spill out. Radiate generosity! When you are with others they will sense this and be increased by your generosity. You can be generous with feelings, with talent, with ideas, with sympathy, with support and with your Self.

32
SUPPORT

To give and receive support is necessary in order for us to grow and develop. Much can be achieved alone, but so much more can be achieved through giving and receiving support. In a wider sense, this is how a society grows and evolves. Giving support to others is sometimes difficult, especially if you don't agree with what they are doing. The result, however, will only be positive, for an offer of support is rarely refused and when it is accepted you are creating the right conditions for growth and expansion. When you support others you support yourself.

33
GIVING

The right way to give is to make sure that there are no strings attached, that there will be no later price to pay. Give in this way and you will be repaid many times over for your trouble. Selfless giving is a key to meditation, as it opens up your defences so that the spirit of life can fill you. This is the gain that comes through giving. Try it – give a little of your time freely to someone in need and encourage others to do the same. The more people there are who give in this way, the better will be the quality of life for everyone. Giving is a way of making a contribution to creating a better world to live in.

34
RECEIVING

Can you receive with no strings attached? Can you open yourself so that you can receive gifts? These may come from other people, but in meditation we are talking about the gifts that can come from your inner self. These gifts are intended for you to use in your life, and you will be brought whatever it is that you need at a particular moment in time. It may be insight, inspiration, confidence, ability, strength, love, hope, success or many other qualities. Whatever you need you can receive it from within. None of these things can be found in the material world; they can be found only in people, and like buried treasure they often lie deep. But they are all there in an infinite supply.

35
ANTICIPATION

When you know that something good is going to happen to you but you are not quite sure when, don't miss out on the experience that comes before the event – the anticipation of it. Rather like experiencing a journey for its own sake and not for arriving at your destination, anticipation will spur you on. Knowing that something will happen can often blind us to the present moment, so stay firmly rooted in the present, experiencing every last drop of life that can come from it.

36
FRIENDSHIP

Don't wait for friendship to come to you, but create it by being a friend yourself. To have a friend you must be a friend, and this means going out and doing something about it. Be a friend to yourself; be kind to yourself; give yourself a treat. This may mean taking a break, letting the stress go for a while, meditating quietly so that the messages about what you really need can get through to you. Be a friend to yourself and you will find that your body, mind and spirit respond positively and will certainly not be your enemy.

37
LONGING

Like anticipation (see 35), longing is a feeling that is future-oriented. In meditation this is a distraction, for your attention should be directed to the living moment of the here and now. This attention will not disperse your longing — but try shifting your attention from the future event, the object of your longing, to the experience of longing itself. This will bring you insight into its meaning and also help to dispel any illusions that may be standing in your way.

38
HOPE

Even at the lowest point, there is always hope. It is a human attribute that will always be there, no matter what. Do not shy away from hope, but let it grow, for other things will come from it. Hope is like sunshine to a flower, which will respond to its rays and open its petals to receive it. Hope is very close to the inner source of life, of our very existence. It is a foundation upon which all our aspirations and dreams can be built, so lay the foundation well.

39
DEDICATION

To be dedicated is to open the doors to endless possibilities. Dedication means going to your limit, and at this point you will always find that there is something more, that you can go beyond your limit. The limits that you thought you had will move – you can always do more than you thought possible. To achieve an apparently impossible goal requires dedication, and dedication will lead to the achievement of that goal. Meditate on your own personal impossible goal, your dream. Then meditate on dedication and what this will mean to you. If you want to stay within your known boundaries, that's fine. But if you want to go beyond them, you will need dedication.

40
BRAVERY

Being brave means doing something you know is right but that you would rather not do. Bravery is taking a risk when the result justifies that action. Bravery is acting when the outcome is unsure. Bravery is seeing a task through to its conclusion. It takes courage to be yourself; it is a brave person who does not live a conventional life. Often this particular form of bravery is needed to avoid living a life that cannot flourish. Courage is needed to live an authentic life, one that is true to one's own way or path.

41
NURTURE

Be gentle and careful with yourself. Do not punish yourself in the process of achieving your goal, but nurture the qualities in you that you wish would grow and become stronger. When this part of yourself is undeveloped, it is like a child who needs encouragement and sensitivity – not bullying but nurturing. Nurturing the child within will enable certain qualities to grow and flourish, so be aware of the child's needs from day to day. You can do this in meditation by watching and responding to those needs as they occur to you. The process of nurturing takes place over a period of time; it does not just happen once, but should continue all the time.

42
SELFLESSNESS

To be selfless is to remove an obstacle. Too often our egos are so strong that nothing else can enter our consciousness. To act selflessly means that the ego's boundaries become transparent to the light of greater awareness, and in meditation this is a great boon. Act selflessly, and you will grow in awareness and experience new dimensions to reality. This is a key to expanded consciousness that has been handed down to us from the ancient wisdom of both East and West. To lose one's identity is to receive a greater one. To act selflessly is to open awareness to a greater sense of Self.

43
HONESTY

There are qualities which open up life before us, and there are those which seem to close it down so that all its possibilities become denied to us. A quality which has the effect of opening up a rich life is honesty. In meditation, this means being honest with ourselves. Exploring our inner personalities involves an encounter with our thoughts, feelings and imagination. We must be true to all of these. Beware illusion, and in particular beware the concept of the Emperor's New Clothes. You are exploring your true individuality, and whatever you encounter, whatever is real for you, is what you should remain true to. This may mean that you do not experience the same thing as your friends. This is all right. An experienced meditator is not a sheep.

44
WISDOM

The source of wisdom is experience, for experience brings the ability to make certain judgements about life and to discriminate between right and wrong. When something has just entered awareness it is young and undeveloped, raw and lacking in direction. With experience comes the ability to take this new awareness and create from it something worthwhile and lasting, to take the raw material of consciousness and create from it something of use not only to ourselves but also to other people. It is unwise simply to present the raw material; it should be held until experience gets to work on it. Then what we bring forth will be wise and considered, and other people will respond to us and can learn from us.

45
SENSITIVITY

Through stillness and the ability to listen and watch comes sensitivity. See how much more you become aware of when you become still. To develop sensitivity, speak less and hear more, look less and see more. Suspend your opinions and beliefs for a while so that you can receive the opinions and beliefs of others. Wait for the right moment to act, but until then remain still. Developing sensitivity will enable you to understand better what is being said to you, whether those communications come from within or without. You will know then what you need to do.

46
KINDNESS

Turn to kindness first if you wish to improve your situation, particularly where relationships are concerned. An uncalled for act of kindness, even towards someone antagonistic to you, will turn the situation around. An act of kindness will spur the universe to reward you, although this should not be your motivation for acting thus. If you are down in the dumps, lacking success, depressed at the state of the world, wondering what is the point of it all, I recommend kindness, even if it is just to yourself. The response will far exceed the act and will convert a downward-heading spiral into an upward-moving one.

47
ENDURANCE

Those things that are worthwhile are usually hard won and may have involved a lot of time, commitment and endurance. The quality of endurance in meditation, however, is not the same as physical endurance. In meditation there is no end that endurance will lead you to, nor is there any pain to endure. Endurance here means the ability to see something through to the end, to give it time, to be patient and to wait for the change. Endurance in meditation means accepting that change and insight will come and that any suffering will not disappear but will be transformed. The time before this happens is the time for endurance.

48
SUPPORT

If support does not come to you from outside, you will find it within. There are three forms of consciousness: the first is our everyday consciousness, the awareness of our normal, everyday reality; the second is the consciousness of the imagination and of the dreams that come to us in sleep; the third lies beyond these and is the consciousness of dreamless sleep. From out of this comes all that we perceive to exist – our everyday reality which we inhabit when we are awake. When we sleep, everything disappears back into it. This final reality, the source of everything that we know, is what you can turn to for support. From it all things come, and to it all things return. It is the foundation of our being, and the support on which our lives are built.

49
SOLITUDE

When you are alone with yourself, you are not truly alone. If you can turn your attention in on yourself, you will be in the company of a rich and rewarding world of feelings, thoughts and imaginations. Contact this world through meditation, and you need never be lonely. But we all need a certain amount of solitude, in order to enter our own inner world and obtain sustenance, support and renewal from it. There are many cyclic processes at work in life. One natural process which is often denied is the cycle of solitude. For a while everyone should turn inwards, to be alone with themselves and become renewed. This sense of renewal can then be turned outwards again and everyday life will continue afresh.

50
HEALING

In its true sense healing is not the same as making well, although this may be a consequence of healing. Healing is to make whole, to bring together something that has been divided. In terms of the whole person, this means that when we consider our ailments it is not just the physical body that needs treatment but the living being that is our self too. To heal means to bring the conscious and unconscious selves into relationships, to forge a connection between inner and outer worlds of experience and to build a bridge between mind and body.

51
COMPASSION

Healing brings with it the experience of compassion. When we can understand what is needed to heal ourselves an understanding comes of what may be needed by others, and if other people are suffering we experience their suffering with them. To be compassionate, to understand and suffer with others, is to assist their healing and to relieve them of some of their burden. To heal ourselves requires awareness; to heal others requires compassion.

52
AWARENESS

A state of awareness can come through stillness in meditation. In everyday life we are bombarded by sensations, thoughts and feelings; we are at their mercy to push us around, to make us act without being aware of our reasons. In this situation we are not in control, although we would like to think we are. Finding some time for stillness in the middle of all this daily activity means that we can really stop and listen to everything – every thought, feeling and sensation that is affecting us. Then you can become aware of yourself – and you will be able to respond in the right way and take control of your life.

10

A QUESTION-AND-
ANSWER SESSION

This chapter covers a number of questions that may have occurred to you while reading this book and while practising meditation. Some of the information you will have read already; here it is recapped upon for quick and easy reference and sometimes points are discussed in greater detail. Other topics, however, will only have been touched on briefly elsewhere in the book or will be entirely new.

What is meditation?

In the context of this book meditation is relaxed awareness. The method that I have developed owes a lot to oriental forms of meditation, but there are fundamental differences. The reason for them is to create a form of meditation suitable for the Western mind and lifestyle. The experiences of relaxation and heightened awareness are not unusual – but they are not normally conditions that we experience at the same time. Put them together and you have the basis for what I often refer to as 'the meditation experience'. Two ingredients are needed in order to produce this experience: first, techniques for relaxation; secondly, techniques for creating heightened awareness. This is what the meditations in this book are all about.

A major consequence of this approach is that rather than emptying the mind, as in many oriental methods, the aim is to accept whatever comes into the mind – thoughts, feelings, images, sensations – and to become an observer of them. In this way you become aware of what is going on inside you and can then respond appropriately in your everyday life to improve your situation.

Throughout the book there are overlaps with other approaches to self-awareness – in particular positive thinking, visualisation technique, self-healing and self-hypnosis. For creating the relaxation response I have drawn on systems such as the Alexander Technique and autogenics (see pages 222 and 224 for more information).

What are the benefits of meditation?

Relaxed awareness brings the immediate benefit of being able to control your stress levels. This in turn has a positive effect on health and well-being. The meditation experience is therefore eminently suitable for people with a stressful lifestyle or who are recovering from a stress-related illness. Because meditation is holistic, being concerned with both mind and body and with the relationship between them, the benefits touch on almost every area of life, especially those to do with our relationships. Meditation puts you in touch with your self and your needs, helping you to achieve fulfilment in your life. This means improved relationships both with your inner self and with other people. It brings you into a right relationship with the world in general, so that another significant benefit is to encourage a sense of belonging and a sense of purpose. Far from meditation being an action of withdrawal, it puts you more in touch with the world in which you live.

Are there any negative side-effects to meditation?

The golden rule is that if it feels all right, fine; if not, then don't do it. Meditation should be an enjoyable experience which brings you many benefits. If you find this is not the case, it is not the right approach for you. When you first begin to meditate you might feel insecure or uncertain about its effects, but you should persist because this is normal. If the uncertainty does not diminish, this is a sure sign to stop. Like all things, meditation should be done in moderation – don't overdo it, particularly in terms of the length of time and frequency of your meditations.

How should I arrange my environment when meditating?

In general, it doesn't matter where or when you meditate but certain conditions will be conducive to your meditation experience. As far as your environment is concerned, some simple suggestions are worth keeping in mind. Lighting should not be too bright and the room should be comfortably warm. Try to make sure you are not disturbed and cut yourself off from any intrusive noise (take the phone off the hook, for instance). Wear loose clothing. It helps to build up a sense of ritual by meditating in the same place and at the same time of day. A special chair or meditation mat are often used, and before your meditation you could prepare the space by playing some soothing music and lighting a candle or burning some incense. Try to create a space in which you feel at ease with the atmosphere. You will discover that regular meditation in a room seems to change its atmosphere, so be aware of this and encourage the 'right' sort of atmosphere to develop. I like to have some flowers in the room and you might like one or two special objects – a crystal, for example, or a picture or ornament that has some special meaning for you.

Can I meditate on my own?

Yes, and one of the reasons why I have written this book is to demonstrate that it is possible to meditate successfully on your own. Traditionally it has been thought necessary to have a teacher, but with my method you can be your own teacher.

There are advantages to meditating in a group, just as there are advantages to meditating on your own. On your own, you can go at your own pace and work out your own programme. You are also not tied to meditating at a particular time or in a particular place. In a group, you receive the support of other members and can talk over your experiences. Group meditations require more discipline and a formal structure, and usually have a leader who will guide you through the meditation programme.

Is it all right for children to meditate?

Yes. Sitting or lying still for a length of time might be difficult for a child, but this doesn't matter at all. Children usually have little difficulty employing their imaginations to the full and take to the meditation experience easily. Never force them, and don't expect persistence. I think there are two main benefits for children. First, the mystique is absent from meditation at that age, so they see it as something perfectly natural. Secondly, meditation can in some cases help to calm an over-active child – but it doesn't always work!

Does it matter if my meditation is interrupted?

The only difficulty might be in having a surprise – if, for example, the doorbell goes or someone disturbs you. In general, interrupting a meditation will not matter. For example, if you feel uncomfortable or for any other reason wish to stop meditating before the end of the sequence, simply open your eyes, sit or lie quietly for a few seconds to regain your composure, and then carry on as normal.

How long does it take to learn to meditate?

Learning to meditate is not primarily a question of being taught but of doing it. As soon as you try it for yourself you can meditate, the rest is a matter of experience. Some people take to the meditation experience straight away whereas others need a little encouragement and discipline to stay with it for a while until the results and the benefits become apparent.

Can I create my own programme of meditations?

Most certainly, yes. This book is structured so that you can work your way through it from beginning to end if you like. But feel free to adapt the meditations themselves, and to create your own work programme.

How long should I meditate for?

If you are meditating in a group, this will be determined by the group's programme. If you are on your own, it really doesn't matter – whatever feels comfortable for you. It could be for a few seconds or half an hour. Don't overdo it. There is no need to meditate for long periods of time. Throughout the book I have suggested the length of time that each meditation might take, but these are guidelines only. Meditation encourages you to become more aware of your needs, which include the length of time you should meditate.

How often you meditate is also up to you, but I would suggest once a day. Ideally, try to meditate at the same time each day, so that you introduce a sense of continuity and rhythm into your meditations; but don't worry if you can't. Meditation might make you feel more wide awake afterwards, so last thing at night might not be the best time, although a relaxation programme on its own will be just what you need to help you to sleep. Don't worry if you fall asleep when meditating. You probably need it.

Can meditation relieve stress?

Most certainly it can. Meditation enables you to reduce unhealthily high levels of stress and then control it. A certain amount of stress, at the right level and at the right time, can be a positive benefit, enabling you to achieve a goal which might need motivation and willpower. But too much stress can damage your health, and will at the very least have an adverse effect on your quality of life.

What is the best posture for meditation?

There are two main criteria. The first is that your posture should be comfortable, and the second that you should not be cramped up or slouched which would affect your breathing. Lying on your back is suitable. If you sit, make sure that your back is straight and well supported. You should aim for the sensation of feeling poised as well as relaxed. Yoga postures are suitable, but not necessary. It helps to have a good stretch before you adopt a posture, as this helps to release any tension and prepare you for becoming aware of the messages coming to you from your body. Become aware of these, and you are on the way to moving into the correct posture for you.

Avoid wearing jewellery or anything that might be distracting or which could constrict you. Wearing loose clothing is a good idea too.

What is the Alexander Technique?

It is a system which suggests that the way we are is reflected in the postures that our body adopts. It follows from this that if we want to change ourselves, it is possible to do it by changing postural habits. This means becoming aware of the way we move, sit, lie or stand, and then changing them through appropriate exercises. Frederick Matthias Alexander, born in 1869, was an actor but had a speech problem – he sometimes lost his voice on stage. This led him to study his own patterns of body use. He focused in on what he called the primary control – the correct positioning of the head in relation to the spine, which is made possible by relaxing the neck. Good posture follows from understanding the primary control. The principles of the Alexander Technique bear some similarity to instructions on Zen meditation and poised posture.

What is the correct way to breathe in meditation?

Make sure that you are not slouching, which crushes your abdomen and makes it difficult for you to breathe deeply and easily. Meditation starts with controlled breathing. You should breathe slightly more deeply than normal, rhythmically (counting breaths helps), and deep down into your abdomen so that your diaphragm can expand and contract freely and easily. Begin the meditation by being aware of your breathing. Then continue to breathe in a free and open rhythm. You will eventually cease to be aware of your breathing as a focal point for your awareness, unless you deliberately choose to maintain this awareness.

What is the easiest way to relax?

The easiest way is by controlled breathing. You can do this at any time, at any place. Simply breathe slightly more deeply than you would normally and let any tension flow out from you as you breathe out. You could also say to yourself, 'I am relaxed', or simply the word 'Relaxed' or 'Calm', as you breathe out. It works, especially if you are nervous about something like an exam, an interview or a visit to the dentist.

What is the relaxation response?

It is the body's response to mental suggestions that you relax. Human beings are suggestible creatures – give us the right suggestions and we respond accordingly. In this way the relaxation response is created not by you doing anything in a physical sense but by giving yourself the right suggestions, in this case the suggestion to relax. In addition, the relaxation response can be encouraged by creating the right conditions for it to happen; posture in particular is important.

What is a mantra?

To help focus the mind, an object for meditation is often employed. A mantra is just such an object, but rather than being a physical object it is a word or phrase repeated either out loud or to oneself. An image or picture which is used as a suitable subject for meditation is called a yantra.

I use a mantra for meditation, but rather than making it something mystical or esoteric I use clear statements. You can choose your own, depending on what you would like to achieve. The mantra is combined with positive thinking to create a mental device which not only helps to focus the mind but also has a positive effect, for example, encouraging self-confidence, improved memory or performance at a particular task.

What is autogenics?

It is an effective relaxation technique which was developed by a German psychiatrist, Johannes H. Schultz, in the 1920s. Although it was originally developed as a therapy, its applications are much wider. It employs a mixture of auto-suggestion and self-hypnosis and is basically a self-help relaxation programme; the auto-suggestions are given in a certain order and their phrasing is important. The principles of autogenics are easy to learn and apply. You direct your attention away from the external environment and focus on body sensations of heaviness and warmth, which encourage muscular relaxation. The use of autogenics is accepted more in Europe than in Britain and the USA, but its popularity is growing.

What are personality types?

How you respond to meditation will depend partly on what type of person you are. It might be just what you need, or it might not be the right approach for you. Meditation itself will help you to understand yourself better, to become more aware of what sort of person you are.

Centuries ago personality types were divided into four basic categories: melancholic, sanguine, phlegmatic and choleric. These four types are still valid in homoeopathic treatment, in which treatment is prescribed not just on the basis of physiological symptoms but on personality 'symptoms' too.

There is a modern correspondence in Jungian psychology, which recognises four personality types: thinking, feeling, intuitive and sensing. These in turn correspond roughly to the astrological elements of Air, Water, Fire and Earth respectively. Indeed, astrology goes even further and moots twelve basic types, each represented by a sign of the zodiac.

The subject of personality types could make a book in itself, but for our purposes it is enough to say that it is a subject well worth looking into to gain more insight about yourself, your behaviour, the way other people respond to your behaviour and so on. It is also helpful in deciding what will be most effective for you, and what approach to meditation you should adopt.

What role does ritual play in meditation?

In any ceremony, ritual gives a sense of rhythm and pattern to life. It also gives a background within which the real action and experience can take place. The same applies in meditation. Developing a sense of ritual means that you have a structure within which to work. The ritual itself is much less important than what happens within it — what the actual experience is for you. It is easy to get caught up in a ritual if it becomes over-elaborate, so keep it as simple as possible. There should be just enough to create a structure to your meditation within which you can work, and within which the meditation itself can work.

What are the physiological effects of meditation?

The effects include a decrease in your heart rate, blood pressure, breathing rate, oxygen consumption, metabolism, blood lactate, blood cortisone levels, brain-wave frequency and muscle tension. There is a particular relationship between muscle tension and levels of mental anxiety. The first stage in relaxation and meditation is often that of focusing on and then controlling your breathing. This in turn has an effect on the flow of oxygen into the bloodstream, and thus an effect on your heart rate and other associated functions. The assumption is that there is a relationship between mind and body; in meditation you set out to explore this relationship and develop it, so that mind and body are working in harmony and not antagonistic to each other.

What is visualisation?

Visualisation is the deliberate process of forming mental images or pictures. The effect is similar to dreaming, but whereas dreams happen to us, visualisation is something over which we can exercise some control. In just the same way that dreams are messages from the unconscious, the images created in visualisation can also be interpreted to reveal insights about our inner selves. The aim is not to be totally in control of visualised images, but to set a scenario and then let the unconscious take over and change the images as it will. You can then become an observer and allow the images to change, grow and develop. The power of this technique lies in the ability to choose what it is that you would like to explore, and then let the unconscious do the work for you. Just as dream images need interpretation, so too do visualised images. They should be treated not literally but as symbols whose meaning needs to be allowed to unfold.

What is the unconscious?

This is an impossible question to answer definitively, but in the context of this book I mean it to be everything inside

ourselves that is not within the boundaries of waking awareness. The unconscious can be regarded as having an objective
reality, one which exists within us. It is the source of all our
waking experiences, thoughts, feelings, imaginations, sensations; the storehouse of memory, and, perhaps even more
significantly, the source of all our behaviour patterns. Just as
there appears to be an objective outer world, the unconscious
can be treated as an objective inner world; it is this with
which we seek to form a relationship through meditation, to
discover, experience and learn about our unconscious, inner
life. The ego, our waking awareness, is rooted in the unconscious. It is the ground of our being.

What is the ego?

It is the present conscious personality: the 'I' as we ordinarily
know it.

What is a symbol?

A symbol is an image or object which carries a much deeper
meaning than lies on its surface. A symbol connects us with
the unconscious, and the meaning of the symbol can change
and develop as it is fed by the unconscious. In other words, a
symbol is not fixed but can change and grow.

How to interpret symbols is a tricky question because,
although there are commonly accepted interpretations (that
is, archetypal interpretations), there is a large personal
element involved too. This means that no one can tell you
what a symbol means for you, but that you must make your
own interpretation, depending on how you feel about it and
how you relate to it. The right way to interpret the symbols
in dreams and visualisations is simply to live with them and
let their meaning unfold for you in time, although you can
help this process along by discovering the archetypal interpretations. You will experience a growing awareness of
what your symbols mean, or you might have flashes of

insight or inspiration. Sharing your inner images with other people is a good way to amplify their meaning, as is keeping a record of your experiences.

What is an archetype?

Archetypes are unconscious patterns of energy and behaviour, and have properties which are shared by everyone in every culture. They often manifest in dreams and visions, taking the form of universal symbols and images. To the degree that we are unaware we can be driven by their power. If, however, they are met and confronted consciously, as in meditation, we can learn to relate to them and use their energies creatively, becoming more fully conscious and whole. An archetype can manifest as an unconscious pattern of behaviour. Quite literally the gods of the ancient world can now be understood as archetypes. Perhaps they no longer live up Mount Olympus, but they continue to live within us. Venus, for example, is the way we conduct our relationships, Mars is the aggression and willpower that lie within us, and so on.

What is positive thinking?

If a thought is placed in a human mind, that person will respond to it. So why not deliberately place positive thoughts in the mind so that we respond positively? This is the basis of positive thinking. The aim is to feed the unconscious with thoughts that tend to boost us up rather than knock us down. The technique can be successfully applied in meditation. Choose a positive thought that is appropriate for your own situation or needs and then use it like a mantra (see page 224), repeating it to yourself in your meditation. If you keep telling yourself that you are a worthless, useless person your unconscious will eventually come to believe it and respond as if you are; but tell it that you are confident and competent, and it will respond accordingly. Your behaviour patterns will change in just the right way to reinforce your desired aim of developing confidence and competence, for example. Positive thinking works – try it!

What is an affirmation?

An affirmation is a mental suggestion used in meditation as a way of reinforcing positive thinking.

Are dreams stimulated by meditation?

Dreams are messages from the unconscious written in symbolic language, and our relationship with them is difficult to pin down. They usually occur when there is some need for the unconscious to try to affect or modify our conscious behaviour. (We dream several times during a period of sleep, but those dreams that we remember are in the minority. Whether we remember our dreams or not, they work their effect on us. Those that we remember we tend to regard as most significant simply because we do remember them.)

I don't know whether or not dreams are stimulated by meditation, but what I do know is that meditation, particularly with visualisation, is dealing with exactly the same process as that of dreaming. Our attitude towards understanding visualised images and the way they unfold should be the same as the way we interpret dreams and experience their effect on us. You can also incorporate your dream experiences into your meditations by recalling images that you remember or which seem particularly significant. Try recalling and meditating on your latest dream.

Should I keep a diary of my meditation experiences?

This is an excellent idea for several reasons. The process of writing down your experiences will encourage you to expand on their meaning for you – realisations and ideas will crop up as you write. Rather like dreams, the memory of meditations can dim very quickly; so writing down your experiences grounds them for future reference. In time you will uncover patterns of development. Frequently some later event has a direct bearing on a particular meditation experience, so if you keep a record you will be able to refer to it. (Realisations about the meaning or significance of a particular experience can come much later than the experience itself. The imagination or symbol, comes first, the understanding later.)

What are the chakras?

The ancient Hindu sacred texts called the *Upanishads* describe seven main centres of consciousness, the control centres for all the different functions and experiences of the human being (see illustration on page 68). The main chakras are the crown, brow, throat, heart, solar plexus, sacral and base of the spine. The system of chakras has been incorporated into Western culture and also modified, for example by associating the rainbow colours with each of the chakras. I find the system useful in helping to focus on different facets of awareness, so I have developed meditations associated with each chakra that enable you to choose a particular area that you would like to work with. What we know about the associated chakra helps to deepen the meditation experience by feeding into it appropriate colours, images and ideas. The chakras provide focal points for the meditation experience. In more esoteric terms, the chakras are psychically receptive and active energy centres interpenetrating and affecting the physical as well as the subtle bodies, the link with the physical being through the endocrine system.

What are correspondences?

In astrology, an association can be made between any object or experience and a sign of the zodiac when they have some quality in common. For example, the sign of Pisces is associated with poetry, so anything poetic is said to correspond with Pisces. Anything that you care to mention comes under the rulership of a particular sign of the zodiac, or corresponds with it. This system of correspondences is useful because if some flower, crystal, colour, emotion, herb, metal, career, part of the body and so on has some significance for you (perhaps cropping up in a meditation), then you can find out more about its meaning by reading about the corresponding sign of the zodiac.

Correspondences are central to systems which map out the relationship of mind, body and spirit, or between the inner and outer worlds of experience. For example, each of the seven chakras has correspondences such as the colours that I use in the meditation experience. Another example is in alchemy, where each of the planets corresponds with a particular metal: gold/sun, silver/moon, mercury/Mercury, copper/Venus, iron/Mars, tin/Jupiter and lead/Saturn.

What are colour meditations?

Different colours have different effects on us: for example, red can be stimulating whereas blue can be calming. The colours that we like and dislike can be interpreted to give insights into our psychological state of mind. These principles are used in meditation when colours are selected to create specific effects. Also, colour correspondences – in this book correspondences with the chakras in particular – enhance our understanding of the right way to use colour in meditation to produce a required effect, such as increasing energy or calming nervous tension.

What is meant by holistic healing?

It is an approach to healing whose central principle is that there is a relationship between mind and body. If you are in need of healing it is likely that you have an imbalance in this relationship. Holistic healing treats the whole person, mind and body. Whereas what is known as allopathic medicine treats the body, meditation is one way to approach healing from the direction of the mind.

How is meditation healing?

Meditation does not just focus on one aspect of your being but makes you aware of your thoughts, feelings and body sensations, and the relationship between them. This is one of the main ingredients of holistic healing – becoming aware of yourself as a whole person and finding out what your needs are to keep mind, body and spirit in a mutually supportive relationship. In the context of meditation I talk about this in terms of the relationship between the conscious self and the unconscious. Not only can meditation help you to discover what you need in terms of healing, but it is a way of stimulating the healing process, primarily through relaxation and stress relief; on a deeper level it does so by harnessing the properties of colours, crystals, healing symbols and positive thinking.

What is an inner relationship?

It is the relationship between the conscious self, or ego, and the unconscious.

What does polarity mean?

It means opposites which together form a whole. For example, day and night is a polarity. In the context of the meditation experience the most significant polarities are mind and body, inner and outer worlds of experience, and the unconscious and conscious self. Polarities are often expressed as being either 'masculine' (outgoing, extroverted, active, creative) or 'feminine' (receptive, introverted, passive, nurturing). The Chinese Yin/Yang symbol is an accurate image of polarity.

The Chinese Yin/Yang symbol describes
polarity and the relationship between opposites.

What are crystal meditations?

Different crystals are said to have different healing
properties. As well as, or instead of, using a crystal extern-
ally, it is possible to visualise a particular crystal in order to
work with its special energy. Rather like the colour meditations, you choose a particular crystal to work with,
depending on its unique healing properties, and then meditate
on the image of that crystal, sensing the energy field that it
emits and the effect that it has on you. Correspondences (see
page 230) are employed to gain insight into the right crystals
to choose and the effects that they will create.

What is syncronicity (as opposed to synchronicity)?

Synchronicity (with an 'h') means occurring at the same time.
But syncronicity (without an 'h') is a Jungian term which
means a special sort of coincidence, with a significant
meaning for the person who experiences it. Syncronicity
seems to happen frequently in meditation. Events conspire to
link up with the inner experience in meditation, particularly
with the symbols that crop up in visualisation. When syncronicity happens the events can occur simultaneously, but this
is not a necessary condition. The important thing is that

seemingly simple coincidences suddenly become full of meaning and purpose. The more your meditation experience deepens, the more you will experience syncronicity, until little seems to happen by chance and all of life's events become full of meaning for you. For example, one day while meditating you realise that you need the support of other people. The next day a friend rings you unexpectedly and suggests that you both form a meditation group. That is syncronicity.

What is an inner journey?

When you employ the visualisation technique in meditation you first set up a particular image or scene. Then, if you let the unconscious take over control of the image, it will change, develop and grow. This is what is meant by an inner journey. Quite literally it can be a journey – up a mountain, through a forest, along a river – and as you travel you will meet with different experiences. After you have finished your meditation you can return to it later and continue the journey through to its conclusion. Rather than simply watching the journey unfold in your imagination, you experience it as if you were really there, feeling the ground under your feet, able to touch and feel. Because the unconscious is having its say and creating the inner conditions that you experience, one term used to describe the effect is an 'interactive' visualisation. It is an interaction between you and the images, thoughts, feelings and sensations created by the unconscious via your imagination.

What is biofeedback?

It is possible to detect and measure the frequency of the electromagnetic waves emitted by the brain. The frequency of these waves characterises the type of activity that the brain is experiencing. The frequencies of emissions have been categorised into beta waves (13–30 Hz), alpha waves (8–12 Hz), theta waves (4–7 Hz) and delta waves (½–4 Hz). Beta waves are associated with normal activity, the performance of physical and mental tasks. Alpha waves are associated with states of deep relaxation. Theta waves are associated with reverie, with meditation, with dreaming and the states experienced when entering or coming out of sleep. The slowest, the delta waves, are associated with dreamless sleep.

Now to answer the question! Biofeedback is the process of monitoring these wave emissions so that the subject can adjust his or her mental state accordingly to achieve a desired experience. For example, we know that deep relaxation is associated with the alpha waves, so if you try to relax and then find that you produce the alpha rhythms you know that you are doing it right and can go further into the relaxation. In this way, biofeedback can be a tool for teaching relaxation and meditation by giving you a tangible measurement of your performance. If you have the opportunity, try experimenting with biofeedback as the results are interesting and helpful.

What is the significance of alchemy in meditation?

The meditative traditions are normally thought to be either those of the orient, or in the mystical traditions of the great Western religions. However, there is one that is less well known. Centuries ago, alchemy was the search for a substance that would create gold. But many alchemists viewed their search not in material terms but as a spiritual quest: theirs was a search for transformation and enlightenment. Rather than them conducting chemical experiments, they themselves were the experiment. These learned men put a high value on meditation as part of the process of alchemical self-discovery and transformation, and now we in the modern world know something about the psychological meaning of the symbols that they used to describe their experiences. Meditation provides us with the same experiences, which include certain stages, that equate to the stages of the alchemical process.

I have introduced this subject because you might like to explore it further. Alchemy is a source of many insights, not only about the experiences that come in meditation but about the psychological stages of growth that our lives go through.

Is there a mystical or religious side to meditation?

The meditation tradition exists in all of the world's main religions. You might like to explore one of the meditative mystical traditions, as you will learn a lot from it. But it is a misconception that meditation *has* to be mystical in some way – meditation is a natural experience, not a supernatural one.

What is a peak experience?

The psychologist Abraham Maslow used the term 'peak experience' to describe moments of intense transcendental delight. He suggested that the peak experience is regarded as abnormal or at least uncommon, occurring only to a few people. However, he also contended that it should not be uncommon and should be available to anyone. Peak experiences can be encouraged through meditation and, although it is certainly not possible to turn them on and off like a tap, meditation encourages a sense of insight, inspiration, purpose and well-being, all of which are associated with the peak experience.

11

THE COMPLETE MEDITATION PROGRAMME

Throughout the book I have presented a wide variety of meditations in a progressive manner so that you can work your way through them. To help you to do this, a complete summary follows which you can use as the basis of your meditation programme, whether on a daily, weekly or other basis.

The Total Meditation Environment

Before the summary, however, I want to describe a 'total meditation environment' – the room in which you meditate, its furnishings, the use of colour, natural sounds and music, all designed to create an atmosphere which will enhance your meditation experience. There is of course no actual need to create this total environment, but the idea might appeal to you and you could take some of the suggestions and adapt them.

Furnishings

If the environment is for your own use only, choose some items that have particular significance for you and with which you feel comfortable. Cushions, flowers, a crystal or two and some appropriate pictures can be arranged to create a meditative atmosphere. Have a focal point in the room, in the same way that an altar in a church forms a focal point. It could be a small table on which you place a crystal, a candle or some incense. Keep the furnishings simple and give careful consideration to everything that you include.

If you are going to run a meditation group (see page 239), some people will want to sit on the floor, perhaps on a cushion, while others may want a chair, so select ones that are comfortable and encourage your fellow meditators to sit with a supported, straight back. Avoid chairs that creak in response to small movements.

In Chapter 5 I described a method for cleansing the atmosphere in a room and suggested that you use representatives of each of the four elements, salt or a plant for Earth, a candle for Fire, incense for Air, and a small bowl of water for Water. These items could be included in your meditation room so that you can use them in your preparation and cleansing. Having a chime or bell of some sort in the room can also be appropriate for reasons explained in Chapter 5.

Lighting and colours

Don't have bright lighting in your meditation room. Ideally you should be able to control both the level of lighting, perhaps with dimmer switches, and the colour too. This can be achieved with the aid of a special lamp with different-coloured bulbs which can be dimmed independently, so that you can create different effects by mixing the colours. If this kind of lamp is not available, simply use coloured light bulbs and shades in your room. Refer to Chapters 3 and 4 for the effects of different colours. Arrange the lighting so that you can control it easily.

You should also ensure that the colour scheme in your room creates a meditative atmosphere. Avoid bright colours.

A light, neutral colour is usually best, leaving any colour effects to the lighting.

If you are meditating on your own you can have your own preferred colours, but if you are running a group other people may have different preferences. This is another reason for using a basic background that is light but neutral. You should aim to enhance the meditative atmosphere but in a non-intrusive way.

Music

Consider having a sound system in your meditation environment. A host of excellent relaxation tapes and CDs are available, which can be used before a meditation to create a relaxed atmosphere and even during the meditation if appropriate. The right sort of music must be easy listening to the extent that you don't have to listen to it if you don't want to – the kind that just fades into the background. The specific choice is a purely personal matter – you will know what you like and what has the desired effects on other people in your group. Try some music that includes natural sounds, sounds of the sea, a stream, birdsong, rain falling and so on, or even a tape or CD which has no music but just natural sounds. Waves lapping on a beach, for example, can be extremely evocative and soothing. Experiment to find out what type of music or natural sounds help you to relax.

As well as relaxation music, I sometimes enjoy playing pieces by Mozart or Haydn. Their music is an excellent focal point for meditation and not just suitable for creating a relaxed atmosphere.

Running a Meditation Group

Here are some suggestions. Fix a regular time for your meditations, to which you can invite friends and relatives. You might like to advertise an open meditation to which anyone is welcome. You will find that you develop a core group of regulars, with others dropping in as and when they feel like it. Before an open meditation I work out exactly what it is we will be doing and I base the programme on a theme. This might be something to do with the time of year (see Chapter 5) or something appropriate for the particular group of people.

Consider interspersing silent periods of meditation with a guided meditation and a reading or two chosen from a book, poem or an inspirational writing or prayer of some sort. Here is a programme of this kind from one of my own meditation groups:

PILGRIMS' MEDITATION GROUP

PROGRAMME FOR MEETING
Tuesday 31 May, 6.00–7.00 p.m.

1. THE OPENING
'Quiet, Calm, Peace and Stillness'

2. SILENT REFLECTION

3. READING
From *Sacred Sleep* by Scott Cunningham

4. GUIDED MEDITATION
Dream Time

5. SILENT REFLECTION

6. THE CLOSING
'To The Four Elements'

Next meeting, Tuesday 14 June

I always use the same short meditations at the beginning and end of each session. The opening meditation, 'Quiet, Calm, Peace and Stillness' is read out and goes like this:

Place the word 'Quiet' in your mind. Feel for the spirit of Quiet both within and without. Let the word 'Quiet' fade from your mind, so that only its spirit remains.

Feel for the quiet beneath any noise you might hear, underlying each breath that you take. Gradually become one with the spirit of Quiet.

Take the meditation deeper. Place the word 'Calm' in your mind. Experience Calm both within and without. Gradually release the word, so that only the spirit of Calm remains. Calm underlying every thought and breath.

Take the meditation deeper. Place the word 'Peace' in your mind. Meditate on Peace. Let it touch your heart, mind and breath. Peace fills your body within and without. Release the word 'Peace' so that only the spirit of Peace remains.

Become still.

This short, inspirational meditation can be found in Pam and Gordon Smith's *Meditation, A Treasury of Technique* (see Recommended Reading). The closing meditation, 'To The Four Elements', which is attributed to Diane Mariechild, is also read out and runs:

Creation of Fire, let me unite with you that I may have passion and power.

Creation of Water, let me unite with you that I may have fluid movement.

Creation of Air, let me unite with you that I may have wisdom and intuition.

Creation of Earth, let me unite with you that I may have stability and steadfastness.

The theme for this particular meeting was dreams. In the guided meditation, which I always begin with a relaxation sequence, I invited the group to picture themselves in a temple. They were then to experience themselves moving into a special part of the temple that was kept for 'dream incubation' – a place to go and ask for a special dream to come to them. They were asked by me to imagine that after entering this place they fell asleep and received a significant dream, perhaps a healing dream or one that would solve a particular problem. During the remainder of the meditation the group was given a quiet time in which to contemplate the experience of the temple and the dream, and to meditate on its significance.

After your own meetings, allow time for discussion of the experience and also for chatting and socialising. When I organise a meditation group at times of the year dedicated to particular festivals, I try to turn it into a social occasion by providing some food and drink afterwards.

Finally, don't think that you have to be an experienced or qualified meditator to run your own group. All you need is the desire to do it and a fair helping of common sense. A group needs someone to act as a focal point and to decide on the programme, the practical details and so on. As long as you have a little confidence there is no reason, on the basis of what you have learnt in this book, why you should not go ahead and start your own group. You will have a lot of fun doing it, will meet some interesting people, and will certainly receive support and encouragement, all of which will make your own meditation experience that much more worthwhile.

Meditation Programme Summary

You should experiment to find out which meditations are most effective for you, and you should also be selective, choosing those that are appropriate for your situation. You may, for example, only be interested in relaxation and stress relief rather than going deeply into the visualisation and inner-journey meditations. In this case the relaxation sequences, the quotations in Chapter 8 and meditations in Chapter 9 would be most appropriate. If you are interested in healing, then focus on the colour and healing meditations in Chapters 3 and 4.

Although I have devised a system that you can work through from beginning to end, don't be afraid to 'mix 'n' match'.

Basic relaxation technique (page 5).

Observing Oneself: a relaxation technique that involves observing your thoughts, feelings and sensations (page 8).

Counting Breaths: using your breathing for relaxation and making you aware of inner, unconscious processes (page 10).

The Perfect Posture: moving into the most effective posture (page 12).

The Inner Workspace: creating an inner space within which to conduct further meditations (page 16).

Autogenic Relaxation Programme: a comprehensive relaxation sequence (page 17).

Creating Inner Space: the first full meditation/relaxation sequence (page 25).

Entering the Forest: a visualisation sequence (page 29).

Positive Thinking: a technique for achieving your aims with the use of a mantra (page 43).

Capturing the Moment: a technique for entering the meditation experience (page 45).

The Garden: creating an inner landscape within which to work on your meditations (page 46).

It has given me a great deal of pleasure to write this book and to share my experience and ideas with you. I hope that in turn your own meditation experience grows and blossoms to give you as much life-enhancing pleasure as it has given me. I wish you well.

RECOMMENDED READING

Anderton, Bill, *Life Cycles*, Foulsham, 1990

Baring, Anne and Cashford, Jules, *The Myth of the Goddess*, Arkana 1993

Bloom, William, *Meditation in a Changing World*, Gothic Image, 1987

Bloom, William, *Sacred Times*, Findhorn, 1990

Cade, Maxwell C. and Coxhead, Nona, *The Awakened Mind*, Element, 1979

Crompton, Paul, *The Art of Tai Chi*, Element, 1993

Cunningham, Scott, *Sacred Sleep – Dreams and the Divine*, Crossing Press, 1992

Fontana, David, *The Meditator's Handbook*, Element, 1992

Fontana, David, *The Elements of Meditation*, Element, 1991

Gawain, Shakti, *Creative Visualisation*, Eden Grove, 1978

Harding, D. E., *On Having No Head*, Arkana, 1986

Harp, David, *The Three-Minute Meditator*, Piatkus, 1993

Harrison, Eric, *Teach Yourself to Meditate*, Piatkus, 1994

Hay, Louise L., *You Can Heal Your Life*, Eden Grove, 1984

Hayward, Susan, *A Guide for the Advanced Soul*, Ashgrove, 1984

Herrigel, Eugen, *The Method of Zen*, Arkana, 1988

Hewitt, James, *The Complete Relaxation Book*, Rider, 1982

Holbeche, Soozi, *The Power of Gems and Crystals*, Piatkus, 1989

Hollis, James, *The Middle Passage*, Inner City Books, 1993

Humphrey, Naomi, *Meditation, the Inner Way*, Aquarian, 1987

Humphreys, Christmas, *Concentration and Meditation*, Element, 1992

Jessel, Charles, *An Anthology of Inner Silence*, Pilgrim, 1990

Levine, Stephen, *Guided Meditations, Explorations and Healings*, Gateway, 1992

Liu, Da, *T'Ai Chi Ch'Uan and Meditation*, Arkana, 1986

Macbeth, Jessica, *Moon over Water*, Gateway, 1990

Macbeth, Jessica, *Sun over Mountain*, Gateway, 1991

Markham, Ursula, *Managing Stress*, Element, 1989

Ozaniec, Naomi, *Elements of the Chakras*, Element, 1992

Paladin, Lynda S., *Ceremonies for Change*, Stillpoint, 1991

Peiffer, Vera, *Positive Thinking*, Element, 1989

Schulman, Neville, *Zen and the Art of Climbing Mountains*, Element, 1992

Sky, Michael, *Breathing*, Bear, 1990

Smith, Pam and Gordon, *Meditation, a Treasury of Technique*, Daniel, 1989

Tzu, Lao, *Tao Te Ching* (Richard Wilhelm edition), Arkana, 1985

Wilde, Stuart, *Affirmations*, White Dove, 1987

Wills, Pauline, *Colour Therapy*, Element, 1993

If you would like to find out about workshops and seminars run by Bill Anderton, or would like him to come and present a talk or workshop in your area, please write to him at Pilgrims, 1A College Court, Gloucester, GL1 2NJ, enclosing a stamped addressed envelope. Information about *Crystal Clear*, a meditation tape by Bill Anderton, can also be obtained from this address.

INDEX